An Atlas of
MASSACHUSETTS RIVER SYSTEMS
Environmental Designs for the Future

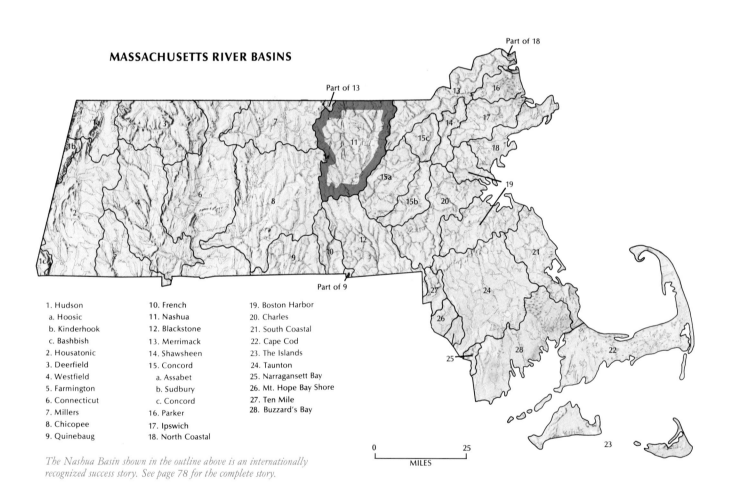

MASSACHUSETTS RIVER BASINS

Part of 18

Part of 13

Part of 9

1. Hudson
   a. Hoosic
   b. Kinderhook
   c. Bashbish
2. Housatonic
3. Deerfield
4. Westfield
5. Farmington
6. Connecticut
7. Millers
8. Chicopee
9. Quinebaug

10. French
11. Nashua
12. Blackstone
13. Merrimack
14. Shawsheen
15. Concord
   a. Assabet
   b. Sudbury
   c. Concord
16. Parker
17. Ipswich
18. North Coastal

19. Boston Harbor
20. Charles
21. South Coastal
22. Cape Cod
23. The Islands
24. Taunton
25. Narragansett Bay
26. Mt. Hope Bay Shore
27. Ten Mile
28. Buzzard's Bay

0   25
        MILES

The Nashua Basin shown in the outline above is an internationally recognized success story. See page 78 for the complete story.

An Atlas of
MASSACHUSETTS RIVER SYSTEMS
Environmental Designs for the Future

Edited by
WALTER E. BICKFORD
and
UTE JANIK DYMON

Published for the
Massachusetts Department of Fisheries, Wildlife &
Environmental Law Enforcement

Amherst
University of Massachusetts Press
1990

PHOTOGRAPHY CREDITS

Ellie Buford - 11, 21, 27 below, 29 above left, below right, 31, 48 left,
50, 78, 79 below right, 85

Bill Byrne - 13, 19, 22, 23 below, 24, 25, 26 above, 28, 29 below left,
above right, 30 below right, 34 above, 36 below,
38 above, 42, 44, 54 right, 58, 64, 66, 68, 79 left, 80

Dennis Connole - 52 left

Bruce Sorrie - 26 below, 27 above

Jack Swedberg - 30 left, 34 below, 46, 48 right, 56, 60 left, 79 above

Peter Trull - 74

Blackstone River Watershed Association - 52 right

Deerfield River Watershed Association - 40

SU-AS-CO Watershed Association - 54 left

Westport River Watershed Association - 23 above

Department of Environmental Management - 32, 60 right

Division of Marine Fisheries - 30 above right

National Park Service - 36 above

Natural Heritage & Endangered Species Program - 38 below, 76

Harvard University's Harvard Forest Diorama - 17

Trout Unlimited - 72

Massachusetts Southeast Regional Planning Commission - 70

Cover photos by: Ellie Buford
Bill Byrne
Jack Swedberg
Natural Heritage & Endangered Species Program

Dedicated to
ANTHONY M. RODRIGUEZ
for his vision, his commitment, his clarity of thought
and his valued, gentle guidance in our efforts to protect
Massachusetts' great natural heritage

FOREWORD

Originally conceived at the Massachusetts Department of Fisheries, Wildlife & Environmental Law Enforcement (DFWELE) under the direction of Walter E. Bickford, this volume emerges as a major study of the river systems of our state and their importance to the future of its environment. It is clearly a book for all who use, manage, or value our remarkable rivers.

As the concept of the volume grew, it became evident that DFWELE would benefit enormously from a collaboration in research, cartography, and preparation of the book with the University of Massachusetts at Amherst. Therefore, the resources of the University's Department of Geology and Geography were placed at the disposal of the project under the skilled guidance of Dr. Ute J. Dymon as Principal Investigator.

To help finance these labors, as well as to meet the costs of producing so comprehensive and handsome a volume, Digital Equipment Corporation, a computer company known for its commitment to the environment, stepped forth. Lou Gaviglia, Vice President of U.S. Manufacturing, and Pete Kinney, Westminster Site Plant Manager, loaned the services of Digital's established environmentalist, Community Relations/Communications Manager Ellie Buford, to assist with the volume and to forward the cause of river and environmental protection both at home and abroad.

The results of this extraordinary combination of talents and resources are plain to see as the reader turns the pages that follow. Here is a full account of Massachusetts' river corridors: their watersheds; their locations; their critical role in maintaining Massachusetts' healthy natural heritage of fish and wildlife; their many other values to the state's environment, culture, and economy; and, most of all, what needs to be done to restore and strengthen these critical lifelines, the state's natural infrastructure. The double-page spreads showing our river basins form the fascinating heart of this story. I commend it wholeheartedly to all readers, whether they use our river systems for fishing, canoeing, hiking, swimming, skating, hunting, bird-watching or any other form of outdoor enjoyment.

To assemble such a volume required the services of many persons. At the University of Massachusetts, Dr. Dymon received her principal assistance from Roy R. Doyon, manager of the Geology and Geography Department's Cartographic Laboratory, and Nancy L. Winter, a writer and style editor. Researchers from the University of Massachusetts included Maxine G. Smith, Joseph T. Errico, and Carl E. Mailler. Cartographic tasks were performed by Dwight M. Harrison, Dorothy A. Graaskamp, Barton J. Wright, Elizabeth Arriaza, Peter Sutton, and Ronald Bucchino. In addition, Marie Litterer, the Geology and Geography Department's Scientific Illustrator, contributed to this effort.

Special thanks are due to the following individuals within the Department of Fisheries, Wildlife & Environmental Law Enforcement: Robert M. Greco, Judith J. Wagner, and Peter G. Mirick for research, writing, and editing; Anthony M. Rodriguez for writing and editing; and Patricia Swain for research. Merillyn Robinson of Digital Equipment Corporation also deserves credit for editing.

In addition, appreciation is due to Raymond D. Barton of Seven Arts Advertising and Marketing Agency for his professional project coordination and management. His assistant, Richard Bridges, deserves thanks for layout and design. Credit also goes to Cindy Sargent of Seven Arts for typesetting.

Many other people conducted research, provided facts, and did graphic and mapping work on the preparation of this book. From the DFWELE's Commissioner's office: Robert W. Austin, David G. Gabriel, Stephen T. Johnson, and Vincent J. Antil. From DFWELE's Division of Fisheries and Wildlife: Wayne F. MacCallum, Peter Oatis, Thomas French, David B. Halliwell, Henry Woolsey, Bruce Sorrie, Scott Melvin, Bradford G. Blodget, James E. Cardoza, and Steven Williams. Working collaboration between DFWELE and UMASS was contracted through the Environmental Institute under the direction of Joseph S. Larson and Elizabeth A. Kidder. Collaboration also took place with Dr. Gwilym Jones of Northeastern University and with Edward Himlan and Randy Showstack from the Nashua River Watershed Association.

In addition, individuals and/or documents from the following agencies and organizations provided valuable information for the book's production: the Massachusetts Audubon Society; the Massachusetts Department of Environmental Protection, Division of Water Pollution Control; the Massachusetts Department of Environmental Management; the Federal Energy Regulatory Commission; the U.S. Department of the Army, New England Corps of Engineers; the U.S. Environmental Protection Agency, Region I; the Charles River Watershed Association; the Nashua River Watershed Association; the Harvard Forest of Harvard University; the Pennsylvania Fish Commission Adopt-A-Stream Program; the Izaak Walton League of America Save Our Streams Program; and Trout Unlimited.

Finally, this book would never have been published without the initial inspiration and conceptual understanding provided by Dr. Larry D. Harris of the University of Florida and Dr. Richard T.T. Forman of Harvard University.

From all those hands came this unique atlas. It is not unreasonable to suppose that Henry David Thoreau would be astonished and pleased to see a copy.

Joseph Duffey, Chancellor
University of Massachusetts

TABLE OF CONTENTS

I. WHY A BOOK ON RIVERS?

"We shall delineate with correctness the great arteries of this great country."

> Thomas Jefferson on the
> Lewis and Clark Expedition   1804

"Someday we are going to improve our navigable inland waters and link them up so as to make a system . . . a land-and-water network which could connect and unify a national recreation ground which would reach from ocean to ocean."

> Benton MacKaye, Shirley, MA
> Founder, Appalachian Trail   1916

"We can tie this country together with threads of green . . . and streams are the most obvious corridors . . . they could link open areas already existing as national and state parks, grasslands, lakes and reservoirs, the entire network winding through both rural and urban populations."

> Final Report of the President's
> Commission on Americans Outdoors   1987

Rivers have played a vital role in the history and making of America as they have with all nations. As the United States grew, visionary leaders and thoughtful citizens articulated the vision of a protected network of river and stream corridors (arteries) which would tie together and enhance the ecological, economic, recreational and cultural amenities of vibrant urban centers with protected wild and scenic areas.

Extensive trail and greenway corridors have been a mainstay of European open space and outdoor recreation for centuries. England alone, for example, has 100,000 miles of hiking trails. The Appalachian Trail was the partial fulfillment of Benton MacKaye's 1916 dream of an American local and interstate trail system. His dream included linear riverway corridors wide enough to provide for fish and wildlife and to give society many benefits.

Early morning on the Nashua River

Rivers, Wetlands and Wildlife

Some of the richest habitats of diverse flora, fish and wildlife are found near the junction of land and water. Riparian corridors consisting of rivers and streams, their beds, banks and floodplains, along with the soils, plants and animals which exist there, are among the most productive biological systems in the world. Greenways along rivers also serve to purify water by filtering surface runoff; they absorb and moderate flood waters, stabilize stream banks and recharge groundwater supplies as well.

Unfortunately, riparian habitat has the dubious honor of being the most abused ecosystem in the U.S. Where once the U.S. had 121 million acres of riparian habitat (land within the 100 year floodplain), today there are only 23 million acres remaining, chiefly because dams were built, rivers channeled and unwise land use practices followed. Massachusetts has lost approximately 50,000 acres of wetlands since 1954 alone, and only 350,000 remain. Much of this remaining wetland is found in riparian corridors that continue to be threatened by increased development.

These remaining premium ecological areas deserve priority protection in their own right. In addition, a rapidly emerging new scientific discipline, called *landscape ecology*, argues forcefully for the ecological need to protect natural areas of adequate size that represent different habitat and natural community types.

Equally important is linking these representative natural ecosystems with protected greenway corridors of adequate width.

According to Dr. Larry D. Harris, Professor of Forest Resources and Conservation at the University of Florida, the necessity for many wildlife species to move freely between a variety of areas, such as terrestrial (upland) and aquatic habitat, is an important basic biological principle. For example, many fish and mammal species such as the black bear, fox, mink and otter move a great deal in their daily and seasonal wanderings. Freedom of movement allows adults to interact, young to disperse and all to obtain food. For these reasons and more, Dr. Harris and other landscape ecologists argue that our numerous parks, wildlife sanctuaries and conservation lands must be made to function as a system, rather than being thought of as islands unto themselves. Corridors of open land which link the state's protected open spaces must be safeguarded against development and become an integral part of the growth planning process. Riparian corridors should be given top priority in open space protection efforts.

Protection of environmental values is just one of the benefits of river corridor protection. Rivers and the land adjacent to them provide opportunities for affordable forms of recreation readily available to local residents. Without having to travel long distances or spend a lot of money, people can enjoy popular forms of recreation such as fishing, hunting, canoeing, hiking, swimming, cross-country skiing and nature observation.

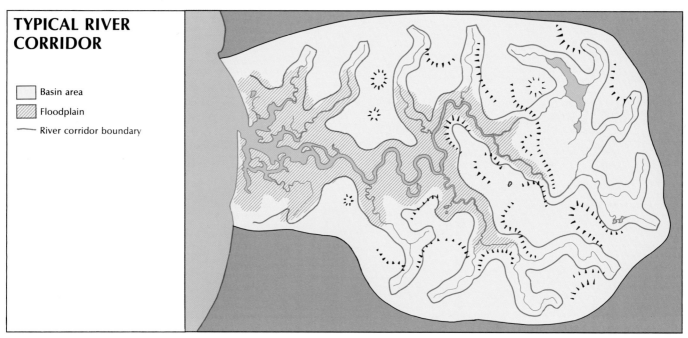

TYPICAL RIVER CORRIDOR

▢ Basin area

▨ Floodplain

— River corridor boundary

A river corridor is the continuous strip of land along both sides of a river. Other names for these linear ribbons of land are riparian corridors or greenways.

River corridor preservation also provides economic benefits. Protected urban rivers or streams often serve as a catalyst and theme for urban renewal and economic revitalization. For example, restoration of the Merrimack River and canal system as part of the Lowell Heritage State Park provided the impetus for an economic revival in that city praised as a model nationwide.

Clearly, a strong economy and a healthy environment go hand in hand when laying the foundation for a high quality of life. River corridor protection efforts focus and give coherence to open space acquisition and land management programs. The goal of protecting river corridors also offers environmentalists, the business community and varied interest groups strong incentives to work together—but the time for effective action is short.

As described later in this book, the basins or watersheds of the state's 28 major rivers may be thought of as ecological units within the state. With river corridor protection as the unifying theme, these basins become logical areas within and around which citizens can organize, plan and act to protect and enhance the ecological, aesthetic and recreational resources of Massachusetts.

This book is designed to show the many values of rivers to our state, to explain how rivers work in the basin ecosystems and to introduce the 28 major river basins one by one. It may serve as an introductory story for those who have not yet become personally acquainted with our rivers and as a reminder for those who know, use and love Massachusetts' rivers and streams.

Wood duck

II. RIVER SYSTEMS

A RIVER SYSTEM is all the land drained by a river and its tributaries from the source of where the river starts, to where the river flows into a larger body of water, its mouth. The rivers and streams of Massachusetts are part of seven major river systems of the Northeast (see map below).

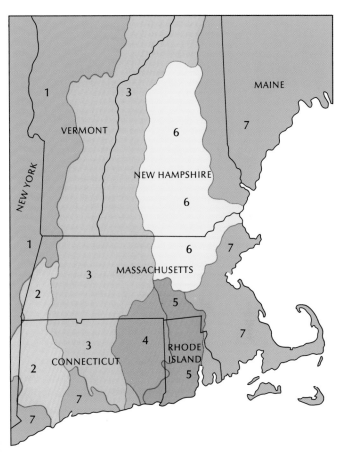

MAJOR RIVER DRAINAGE SYSTEMS IN MASSACHUSETTS IN RELATION TO NORTHEAST HYDROGRAPHY.

1 - Hudson
2 - Housatonic
3 - Connecticut
4 - Thames
5 - Blackstone
6 - Merrimack
7 - Coastal

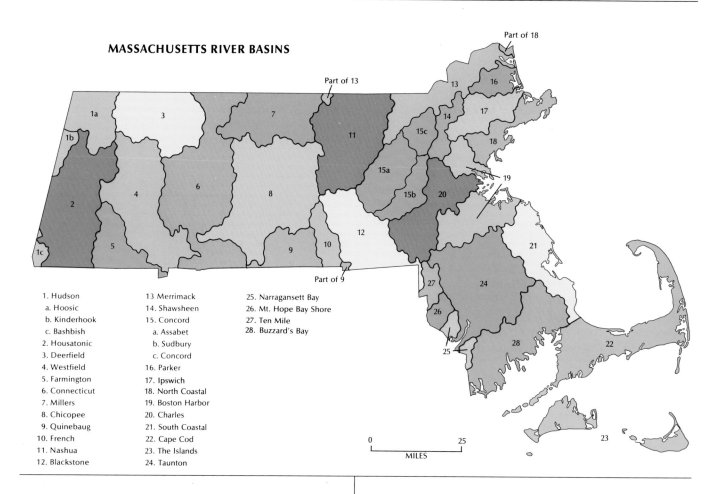

MASSACHUSETTS RIVER BASINS

1. Hudson
   a. Hoosic
   b. Kinderhook
   c. Bashbish
2. Housatonic
3. Deerfield
4. Westfield
5. Farmington
6. Connecticut
7. Millers
8. Chicopee
9. Quinebaug
10. French
11. Nashua
12. Blackstone

13. Merrimack
14. Shawsheen
15. Concord
    a. Assabet
    b. Sudbury
    c. Concord
16. Parker
17. Ipswich
18. North Coastal
19. Boston Harbor
20. Charles
21. South Coastal
22. Cape Cod
23. The Islands
24. Taunton

25. Narragansett Bay
26. Mt. Hope Bay Shore
27. Ten Mile
28. Buzzard's Bay

MILES
0   25

A RIVER BASIN is a particular type of watershed. For the purpose of this book, a basin may be thought of as an ecological unit, or system, as well. All the water, sediment, nutrients and energy eventually flow downhill in a river basin system. The fisheries, other aquatic life, associated forests, vegetation and animals within each basin are dependent on one another to at least some degree.

The smallest streams of a watershed have no tributaries and are called first order streams (1). When two first order streams join, they form a second order stream (2). When two second order channels join, a third order stream (3) is formed, and so on. Orders one and two are often small, steep or intermittently flowing channels, and orders five (5) or higher are larger rivers.

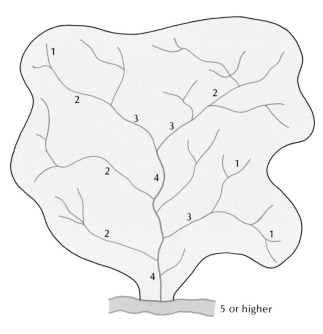

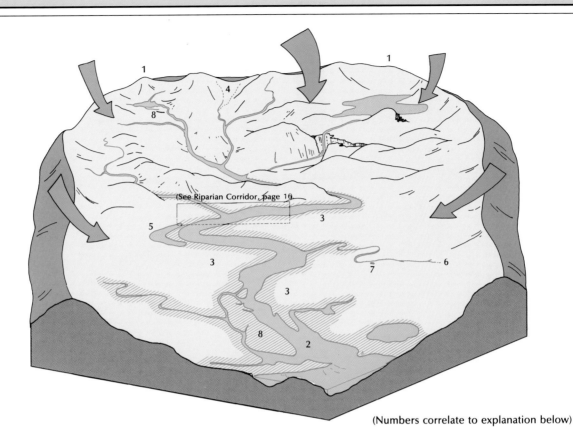

(Numbers correlate to explanation below)

A WATERSHED is a somewhat concave or bowl-shaped catchment basin where precipitation follows the contour of the land to the lower elevations. Most of this water soaks into the soil and becomes part of the groundwater system. The water which does not soak into the soil is called surface water. It runs on the earth's surface into streams, rivers, bogs, swamps or wetlands.

In the United States, the term watershed is often mistakenly used as a synonym for river basin. As water collects at the lowest elevations in a watershed, it does not always form a river. Instead, it may form a lake, swamp, wetland or a groundwater recharge area.

As a watershed naturally captures and channels the precipitation in a given geographic area, it develops many hydrological features (see list of definitions and above diagram).

COMPONENTS OF A WATERSHED

1. DIVIDE: A ridge or elevated land that separates watersheds.

2. ESTUARY: An area where a river flows into the ocean and salt and freshwater mix. Estuarine areas are among the most biologically productive ecosystems in the world.

3. FLOODPLAIN: An area along a river that floods during high water. A 50 year floodplain is the area flooded by a storm that occurs an average of once every 50 years. An invaluable "sponge" for floodwaters, the 50 and 100 year floodplains are often used for deciding land use practices.

4. INTERMITTENT STREAM: Stream channels that only flow seasonally, at snow melt or during rainy periods.

5. OXBOW: A portion of a meandering river cut off by shifts in river flow that leaves an oxbow pond or a complete loop in the river.

6. SEEPS OR SPRINGS: An area where groundwater comes to the surface and soils remain wet even during cold seasons. Seeps are vital feeding places for wildlife during the winter.

7. VERNAL POOL: A temporary body of freshwater that provides crucial habitat for amphibians, crustaceans, aquatic insects and other vertebrate and invertebrate wildlife species. A vernal pool has no predatory fish and, therefore, is an important and safe habitat for rare salamanders.

8. WETLANDS: An area where the ground is low and the soil holds water. Wetlands provide ideal conditions for water-tolerant plants and animals.

DIAGRAM OF A TYPICAL BIOLOGICAL COMMUNITY

Riparian corridors support productive and diverse biological communities, as shown above.

RIPARIAN CROSS-SECTION

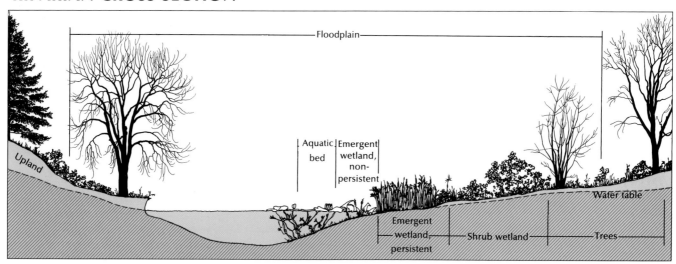

A riparian corridor refers to the land bordering a stream. This land affects the stream in many ways and the stream, in turn, influences these adjacent lands. When used in this book, the term riparian corridor includes the stream, its bed, banks, floodplains, transition zone (between wetlands and uplands) and the adjoining uplands.

III. THE MANY VALUES OF RIVERS: STATEWIDE TRENDS

Ecological Trends / Wildlife History

In many ways, Massachusetts' fish and wildlife appear to be in better shape now than at any other time in the past 300 years. Certainly wildlife suffered enormously in Massachusetts and throughout America after European settlement began. By the 1820's, over three-quarters of the state was cleared of forests for farming and to meet demand for lumber and fuelwood. Even the remaining woodland was used for livestock grazing. Dams and pollution had wreaked havoc with Massachusetts' freshwater fisheries. The final result of this habitat alteration, combined with unregulated commercial hunting, sport hunting, fishing and trapping, was a drastic decline in fish and wildlife populations. Many wildlife species became extirpated (locally extinct) from Massachusetts, and some became globally extinct.

Prior to the Civil War, farmers began to abandon Massachusetts' rocky fields for the fertile lands of the Midwest. As illustrated by the photos to the right, forest cover began to regenerate in lands that were previously cultivated. Eventually, by the 1960's, the land cover in Massachusetts recovered to proportions of approximately three-quarters woodland to one-quarter open land, and the woodlands were no longer grazed. This dense new growth offered excellent habitat for wildlife. With the banning of commercial exploitation of wildlife in the 1890's, and later the regulation of sport hunting and the growth and funding of scientific wildlife and fisheries management, a remarkable resurgence of many of our wildlife species has been achieved (see graph below).

RELATIVE ABUNDANCE

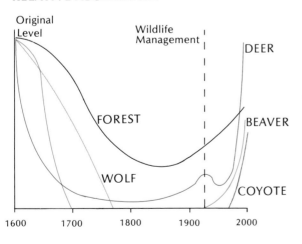

1700 Presettlement Mixed Forest—"The Forest Primeval"

1830 Height of intensive farming. As much as 90% of Massachusetts was cleared of forest cover.

1930 Hardwoods form second crop. Previously farmed land reverts to woodlands and excellent wildlife habitat.

Massachusetts Fisheries and Wildlife Respond Positively to Improved Habitat, Protective Laws and Professional Management

Today, many species that were extirpated or nearly so before 1900 are thriving once again in Massachusetts. White-tailed deer have recovered from less than 1,000 animals in 1900 to over 45,000 in 1989, possibly more than when the Pilgrims landed — and the herd continues to increase. In 1900, there were few resident black bear in Massachusetts. Today, the population is over 750.

Beaver were trapped and driven out of Massachusetts by 1800. Not until 1928 did beaver reappear in a West Stockbridge stream. By 1980, there were hundreds of colonies and thousands of beavers across Massachusetts, some within the metropolitan Boston area. In 1987, despite a harvest of 1,700 beaver by fur trappers, the Division of Fisheries and Wildlife still received over 100 complaints due to costly problems caused by beavers in towns as far east as Route 128.

Beavers, considered nature's engineers, have built hundreds of dams that resulted in flowages (beaver ponds) which are excellent habitat for fish, waterfowl, amphibians and reptiles. Mammals, especially furbearers such as the muskrat, raccoon, otter and mink, move in to take advantage of the excellent habitat and food sources in the flowages. These furbearers are riparian (water-loving) and once again abundant in Massachusetts.

Beavers create flowages that drown trees. The dead trees attract insects which draw pileated woodpeckers and other insect-eating birds. Great blue herons move in to nest in the trees and feed on fish and amphibians in the flowages. In 1986, Massachusetts had 29 known heronries (colonies of heron nests) in which 664 young hatched. All heronries are located in riparian areas with most in beaver flowages.

MASSACHUSETTS WILDLIFE & PLANT SPECIES: A NUMERICAL TALLY BY STATUS (1)

Species / Class	Total	Native Inland	Native Marine or Coastal	Introduced by Man	Natural Range Expansion (2)	Extinct	Extirpated	Potentially Present Inland for Observation(3)	End.*	Th.*	SC*	% Rare	Federally Listed End. & Threat.
		LISTED IN MASSACHUSETTS SINCE 1620						State Rare					
Mammals	94	58	28	8 3 unsuccessful	2 coyote opossum	2 eastern elk sea mink (subspecies)	8	55	7	—	5	14	7 6 whales 1 bat
Birds	434	188 nest annually 40 year round res. 93 predictable annual passage birds (migratory) 19 nest irregularly 129 vagrants (occasional visitors)		5 pigeon starling ring-necked pheasant house sparrow mute swan	25+ turkey vulture mocking-bird cardinal	4 heath hen great auk passenger pigeon Labrador duck	1 gray-cheek thrush	300	9	7	15	14	5 bald eagle peregrine falcon Eskimo curlew roseate tern piping plover
Reptiles	30	24 14 snakes 9 turtles 1 lizard	6 turtles				1 five-lined skink	23	7	4	3	48	6 5 sea turtles 1 Plymouth redbelly
Amphibians	23	22 7 frogs 3 toads 12 salamander	—	1 mudpuppy salamander				23	—	2	6	36	
Fish	78	30	21 11 diad. 10 estuarine (brackish)	27 26 inland 1 diad. 23 reproduce	1 gizzard shad		1 trout perch	56	3	3	3	20.5	1 shortnose sturgeon
Total	659	618		41	28+	6	11	457				18	19
Plants	2,700 approx.			950 approx.			50	2,500	106	80	55	14	2

1. NOTE: Since wildlife is dynamic, these numbers may shift slightly over time (e.g. in the spring of 1989, the bald eagle hatched young in the state for the first time in over 75 years)
2. Natural Range Expansion species are included in Native Inland or Marine columns
3. Complete listings of species in this chart can be obtained from the Division of Fisheries and Wildlife.
* End. - Endangered, Th. - Threatened, SC - Special Concern

Wild turkey were hunted out of the state by 1800. The Division of Fisheries and Wildlife restocked 32 birds in 1972. That initial flock has expanded to over 7,000 birds statewide. Fisher (a large member of the weasel family), mourning dove, wood duck and other species once extirpated from portions of Massachusetts have returned and are flourishing. In the spring of 1988, peregrine falcons hatched eggs, the first in Massachusetts in over 40 years. Bald eagles built two nests at the Quabbin Reservoir in 1988, and eaglets hatched in the spring of 1989, the first hatching in Massachusetts since 1909.

Dozens of vertebrate species unknown in Massachusetts prior to 1900 have naturally expanded their ranges into the Commonwealth or have been introduced by people into Massachusetts. These include: coyote, opossum, turkey vulture, cardinal, large and smallmouth bass, rainbow and brown trout, mockingbird, Norway rat, starling and mudpuppy (a large aquatic salamander). In addition, once decimated native plants have rebounded and many introductions are flourishing.

No Time for Optimism

This apparently encouraging story of wildlife richness is deceptive. Six important vertebrate species formerly found in Massachusetts are globally extinct: four birds (heath hen, passenger pigeon, Labrador duck and the great auk) and two mammals (sea mink and eastern elk). Eight additional mammals, including the most important predators in the pre-European ecosystem, remain extirpated: grey wolf, mountain lion, lynx, wolverine, marten, moose, Indiana bat and fox squirrel. Forty-two species of plants have been lost from Massachusetts. Listed as endangered or threatened are 75 animals (including 34 invertebrates) and 186 plants, and another 87 animals and 55 plants are potentially threatened. This means that over 20% of Massachusetts' native fish species, 30% of the state's amphibians and almost 50% of Massachusetts' reptiles are listed as either endangered, threatened or of special concern. Many of the newcomers mentioned earlier are undesirable and aggressively compete with native species. For example, the purple loosestrife, an aggressive alien plant species, threatens to wipe out the native cattails and drastically alter wetland ecosystems. Wildlife managers strive for *native species diversity* and try to limit introduction of alien species.

More significantly, despite the substantial recovery of once abused habitat, Massachusetts' wildlife face a new and more dangerous crisis in habitat degradation. The development boom which is sweeping the state has the very real potential of causing another cycle of drastic declines in wildlife habitat, populations and species diversity—a decline that will not be reversible.

According to Losing Ground, a 1987 report by the Massachusetts Audubon Society, over 112,000 acres of Massachusetts' open space were lost to residential and commercial development between 1981 and 1987, greater than 20% of all conservation land protected in Massachusetts during the past century. In 1986 alone, 30,000 acres of open space disappeared. By the year 2030, two million acres, or 40% of all the land in Massachusetts, will be developed if present trends of sprawl development continue. Less than half this amount will be protected as open space. An average of only 4,500 acres per year are protected through all conservation efforts in the state, and two-thirds of this is by state agencies.

MASSACHUSETTS IS LOSING GROUND

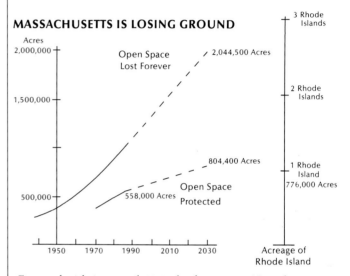

From colonial times until 1970, development in Massachusetts consumed land equal to an area slightly smaller than the state of Rhode Island (776,000 acres). Based on the Massachusetts Audubon Society study, which assumed a slowing rate of development, developed land in Massachusetts will equal an area twice the size of Rhode Island by 2010. By 2030, assuming land consumption trends continue, an area nearly three times the size of the state of Rhode Island—or 40% of all Massachusetts land—will be developed.

Increased development is fragmenting Massachusetts' wildlife lands

Massachusetts Wildlife Needs More Open Space

From an ecological perspective, the four most important characteristics of protected conservation reserves are adequate total acreage, size, configuration and connectivity. If growth and development projections for Massachusetts become a reality, the Massachusetts conservation reserves will be seriously deficient in all these areas.

Total Acreage:

There are over 558,000 acres of conservation land in Massachusetts with an additional 200,000 acres set aside for water supply protection. While seemingly impressive, this represents only 1/10 acre per person. Compared to most states, Massachusetts ranks low on this score. Moreover, Massachusetts' protected open spaces are fragmented in over 5,000 disjointed, oddly-shaped parcels ranging in size from a few acres to the largest of approximately 16,000 acres. By comparison, New York's Adirondack Park is 6,000,000 acres—larger than all of Massachusetts. Vermont's Green Mountain and New Hampshire's White Mountain national forests are also large self-sustaining ecosystems. In some western states, over 70% and up to 81% of land is in public ownership.

Reserve Size:

Many wildlife species need to move daily and / or seasonally. Most daily movement is associated with the need for food, cover and water. Seasonal movement of adult wildlife is necessary for interbreeding to assure genetic variety. Young wildlife also need to disperse to establish their own territories. The approximate home range of a mink or raccoon is 1,000 acres; an otter is 3,000 acres; a bobcat 5,000 acres; a black bear 15,000 acres. These and other species require undisturbed remoteness and solitude found only in large tracts of land. Reptiles, such as turtles, leave riparian areas to deposit eggs in dry sandy areas while some salamander species migrate to vernal pools to deposit eggs. Protection of large reserves is vital to these and other wildlife species.

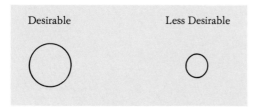

Larger reserves are better able to provide adequate range area for many species of animals in balanced natural communities.

Reserve Shape:

Edge effects occur where two different habitat types meet, such as open fields and woodlands. Some edge effects are undesirable. For example, the parasitic cowbird, which prefers open fields, may invade and replace the eggs in songbird nests located in woodland edges with their own eggs. Domestic pets from developed areas raise havoc with wildlife in nearby reserves. The greater the ratio of edge to area, the greater are the negative edge effects on reserves.

Rounder reserves have smaller perimeters to area ratios and, therefore, less edge effect than oddly-shaped reserves. Black area represents edge.

Connectivity:

Wildlife can exist, at least marginally, in undeveloped areas surrounding reserves. Wildlife can also range between reserves over undeveloped land. However, as open spaces surrounding Massachusetts' conservation reserves continue to become more developed, the reserves become isolated islands and cease to function as a system that can adequately protect wildlife diversity and genetic health. In an ideal situation, development of land surrounding reserves should take into account and provide for wildlife's movement needs. In the absence of such thoughtful development, public agencies need to acquire corridors linking reserves. There are no reserves in Massachusetts capable of maintaining their present level of wildlife species diversity and populations if the open land surrounding them is developed.

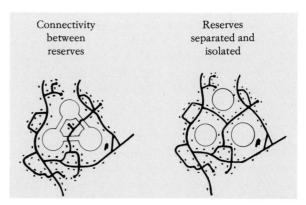

Cluster zoning, condominiums, apartments and other creative land use planning and development can provide the same number of housing units with less impact to open spaces. With careful planning, wildlife and recreational travel corridors can be protected.

Protecting Massachusetts' Natural Heritage

Based on these concepts, the Massachusetts Department of Fisheries, Wildlife & Environmental Law Enforcement has developed a land acquisition policy whose goals are:

1. Enlarge, round out and buffer existing significantly protected wildlife habitat.
2. Link existing protected wildlife habitat with greenway corridors.
3. Acquire endangered species habitat.

River and stream corridors that fulfill these goals are given highest priority in acquisition and protection efforts.

The Ecological, Recreational and Socio-economic Values of Massachusetts Rivers

Ecological:
The following is a brief overview of the status of Massachussetts' flora and fauna and the significance of river and stream corridors to their survival. The statistics and basic facts given are intended to serve as an introduction to readers and to broaden their interest in Massachusetts' wild flora and fauna (specific check lists of the five classes of vertebrate animals may be obtained from the Massachusetts Division of Fisheries and Wildlife). The statistics are subject to interpretation and to change over time. For example, at the inception of this book, three species—moose, peregrine falcon and bald eagle—were extirpated as breeding fauna, although they were all present in Massachusetts. Peregrine falcons and bald eagles have since successfully hatched young. There is also an increase in straggling moose. Archaeological evidence indicates that bison and caribou once existed in the state, but most likely not since Europeans arrived. Therefore, they are not listed.

Swamps and wetlands

Mammals

94 Total species recorded since 1620
28 Marine species (whales, dolphins, seals)
66 Inland species
58 Native - 8 extirpated
  2 Natural immigrants (coyote, opossum)
55 Available for observation - 4 rare
  8 Introduced - 3 failures

River otter

Of the 66 inland mammals listed in Massachusetts, eight were introduced (European rabbit, Eastern cottontail rabbit, black-tailed jackrabbit, European hare, Norway rat, black rat, house mouse and fallow deer). Three of these were unsuccessful introductions—European hare, black rat and fallow deer. Two inland mammals, the coyote and opossum, are immigrants. Eight mammals, including the most important predators in Massachusetts' once balanced natural food chain, have been extirpated from the state (mountain lion, lynx, grey wolf, wolverine, marten, Indiana bat, fox squirrel and elk). Although the moose may be considered extirpated as breeding animals, stragglers from the north are increasing. In 1988, there were 12 known moose in Massachusetts, one of which was female.

As a group, Massachusetts' mammals have gone through the most drastic population fluctuation of all orders of vertebrates. The larger mammals and furbearers were systematically slaughtered to support the needs of the early colonists. The clearing of forests eliminated most of their habitat. By the end of the last century, many of the larger mammals had been extirpated or reduced to pitiful remnant populations that managed to survive in small pockets of thickets and forest. Thanks to the return of our forest habitats, protection from unregulated hunting and trapping and scientific wildlife management, many species have rebounded in this century. Black bear, fisher, beaver, white-tailed deer and otter not only flourish today, but also support annual, carefully regulated harvests by hunters and trappers.

Most of our mammals depend on the habitats provided by rivers, streams, ponds and wetlands. Water-dependent species include mink, muskrat, otter, water shrew, bog lemming and beaver. Many other species, however, spend much of their lives within the habitats immediately surrounding our waterways; they are dependent on mixed upland and lowland habitat. Species in this category include everything from raccoon and deer, which often forage in the water, to our eight species of bats, which often forage on insects above water. All of these species, as well as many others, occasionally use river corridors as travel routes.

Eastern coyote

Birds

434 Total species recorded since 1960
129 Vagrants (occasionally visit state)
4 Extinct (heath hen, passenger pigeon, labrador duck, great auk)
1 Extirpated (grey checked thrush)

300 Likely to be sighted in Massachusetts
40 Nesting, year-round residents
148 Annual migrants which nest in state
93 Annual migrants which do not nest in state
19 Nest irregularly

Osprey

Approximately 300 species of birds can be found and observed regularly during their normal seasons in Massachusetts. While many inhabit upland areas during some portion of their lives, few are not dependent on the habitats provided by river systems and their corridors. The flowing waters of river channels, mudflats exposed during periods of reduced flow, associated swamps, marshlands and river bottom forests all provide valuable habitats for resident and migratory birds.

Massachusetts is located in the "Atlantic Flyway" where three million waterfowl of 17 species migrate north and south each year. The northerly and southerly flowing inland rivers of the state, in addition to the coastline, provide direction, nesting and feeding areas for this great migration. River corridors are also major migration routes for many species of songbirds such as vireos, flycatchers, thrushes, tanagers and wood warblers.

Some species of birds are especially adapted to river life. The Louisiana and Northern water thrushes, for instance, are usually encountered in river corridors. The spotted sandpiper is frequently visible along river bars and shorelines. Many other shorebird species occur along rivers where appropriate mud bars develop. Belted kingfishers patrol rivers from the headwaters to the sea in search of small fish. Osprey (fish hawks) flourish along rivers, and the state's largest nesting group of these birds (over 70 nests) is found on the Westport River. Volunteers have erected special nesting platforms to attract them. The state's many species of herons and bittern depend totally on riparian corridors for food, roosting and nesting sites. The endangered bald eagle frequents riverine corridors in search of fish and roosting areas. In 1988, eagles built two nests at the Quabbin Reservoir and one on the Connecticut River. Birds such as cormorants, night herons and gulls follow river systems for many miles inland in search of good feeding areas.

Rivers and their adjacent landscapes are also critical to Massachusetts' resident waterfowl. Black and mallard ducks and blue-winged and green-winged teal nest and raise their young in the marshes and wetlands along rivers and ponds. Wood ducks and hooded mergansers nest in tree cavities in swampy bottomlands. A less obvious river corridor user is the woodcock, or "timberdoodle," a terrestrial bird which follows and relies on vegetated wetlands within river corridors as its primary feeding and nesting habitat.

River corridors are superb places to view birds because of their open areas contrasting with vegetated edges. Edges where different habitat types meet, such as open water and marshlands, or shrubby areas and river bottom forestlands, are always frequented by birds. Springs and seeps, found at the headwaters of streams and rivers, are important winter food and water sources for many upland birds (including the recently restored wild turkey) because these sites never freeze.

Turkeys at a seep. Wildlife can often find open areas and feed along seeps and streams in winter.

Fish
(freshwater dependent)

78 Total recorded
21 Marine species
57 Inland species
27 Introduced
30 Native species
 9 Rare
 1 extirpated

Massachusetts has 57 freshwater fish species, 30 of which are native to Massachusetts. Some of the more common fish in this category include the brook trout, chain pickerel, yellow perch, brown bullhead and pumpkinseed (a sunfish). The rainbow trout (northwest U.S.), brown trout (European), large and smallmouth bass and white catfish (southern U.S.) are common examples of the 27 species which have been artificially introduced to Massachusetts' inland waters in the last 150 years.

Of the 11 diadromous species (life cycle includes both fresh and saltwater habitats), 9 are native *anadromous* fish, spawning in freshwater, but living primarily in saltwater. Common examples in this category would include the American shad, rainbow smelt, blueback herring, sea lamprey and white perch. These fish provide recreational value to Massachusetts citizens, and some of them provide a substantial portion of the forage base for offshore commercial fisheries. The extirpated Atlantic salmon—considered by many to be the world's premier gamefish—is also in this category and is presently being restored. Coastal Massachusetts has over 100 streams used by anadromous fish. The state Division of Marine Fisheries, in conjunction with local towns, has constructed over 300 fish ladders to assist these fish in navigating past dams to historical spawning grounds. The American shad is the state's primary anadromous gamefish. Thousands of anglers flock to the Connecticut, Merrimack and Indian Head rivers during the shad's spawning run in May and June. The American eel is our only *catadromous* fish, living in freshwater but spawning in saltwater.

Because of the state's geological makeup and northern latitude, natural productivity of inland waters is low, averaging 20 to 40 pounds of fish per acre per year (southern waters produce 60 to 80 pounds per acre). About 5% to 10% (2 to 4 pounds per year) of Massachusetts' freshwater fisheries are comprised of game species such as bass, trout and pickerel. Approximately 30% to 40% are made up of edible panfish species such as perch, sunfish and bullheads. The remainder is composed of baitfish, suckers and other species which have little angling value, but provide

critical food sources for other species and play an important role in their respective ecosystems.

The Division of Fisheries and Wildlife augments the natural productivity of the state's waters by stocking 600,000 hatchery grown trout annually. The division also stocks northern pike, tiger muskie and land-locked and Atlantic salmon.

Despite these programs, the amount and condition of aquatic habitat ultimately determines the abundance, diversity and health of our freshwater fisheries. As with terrestrial wildlife habitat, aquatic habitat loss is caused by pollution and stream corridor manipulation due to development. Subdivisions and changes in ownership often lead to degradation of aquatic habitat and loss of public access as well.

Pumpkinseed (Sunfish)

Despite billions of dollars spent on water pollution abatement, domestic sewage, landfill leachate, industrial toxins, pesticides, and agricultural and domestic lawn chemicals adversely impact all our rivers to varying degrees. Division biologists estimate that 35 to 50 of the 150 "fish kills" (where large numbers of fish die at once due to one cause or another) recorded in the state each year are a result of toxic chemicals discharged into municipal sewage systems or directly into watercourses. Chemical contamination has limited consumption of fish in several major rivers and impoundments.

Despite these continuing serious threats, Massachusetts fisheries are in their best shape in decades. River corridor protection is clearly one of the least expensive and most effective means of safeguarding and improving the health of all fisheries and is required if we are to maintain and improve upon our present level of success.

Reptiles & Amphibians

Reptiles	30 Species recorded
	6 Marine species - all rare listed
	24 Inland species - 14 rare listed
	1 extirpated
Amphibians	23 species recorded - 8 rare listed
	1 introduced

Massachusetts is home to a surprisingly large and diverse assortment of reptiles and amphibians. A total of 23 amphibian species—13 salamanders, 7 frogs and 3 toads—inhabit the Bay State. Combined with 29 species of reptiles—14 snakes, 9 inland turtles, 5 marine turtles and 1 estuarine (salt marsh) turtle — they compose the state's *herpetofauna*. All 53 species are native with the exception of the mudpuppy, a large aquatic salamander which now thrives in the Connecticut River drainage.

Considering the drastic changes in habitat that have taken and are taking place in Massachusetts, it is remarkable that all of our herps have survived. The one exception may be the five lined skink—the only lizard ever recorded in the state—which was apparently extirpated during the last century. Most of the herps have suffered drastic population declines, however, and the trend continues. Fourteen of our reptile species (including 5 marine turtles) and 8 of our amphibians are listed as rare.

The amphibians, which by definition require water or at least damp habitats in order to reproduce, are clearly tied to riverine systems. Some remain restricted to specific river drainages. Most of Massachusetts' frogs, at least one toad and some aquatic salamanders could be maintained by preserving the main channels and backwaters of Massachusetts' major rivers. The preservation of river corridors encompassing considerable upland habitat will be required to maintain other species, for many spend most or all of their lives away from open water habitats. The wood frog and four species of mole salamanders, for instance, breed only in temporary vernal pools and spend their lives on or beneath the forest floor. Corridor protection is also vital to preserve species like the spring salamander which thrive only in cold, unpolluted springs and streams. These delicate systems are easily degraded by clear cutting and development.

The need for river corridor protection is just as vital for the reptiles. Several species, including the musk turtle, snapping turtle, painted turtle and northern water snake, may spend virtually their entire lives in riverine habitats. Other species, such as the Blanding's turtle, spotted turtle, diamondback terrapin and ribbon snake, inhabit wetlands which are usually associated with river systems. All turtles lay eggs and,

hence, even the most aquatic species require upland habitat for their nesting activities. Corridor protection is particularly important for our semi-aquatic wood turtle and the rarest reptile in the state—the bog turtle. The wood turtle spends much of its life in brooks and streams, but it inhabits surrounding upland habitats during the warmer months of the year. The three known bog turtle populations—discovered only in the past decade—appear to require sterile, alkaline fens containing rivulets.

Reptiles and amphibians are far less mobile than birds and mammals. While the latter groups can cross developed areas and recolonize lost ground, often in a matter of years or a few decades, range expansion by herp species is more likely to be measured in centuries. Several of our species reach the northernmost limits of their range in Massachusetts, but without protected corridors of habitat to travel through, they are unlikely to get any further or to return to habitats where they have been extirpated. Unbroken corridors, especially riparian corridors of natural habitat, will be required to insure the continued health and expansion of our species, particularly the amphibians. These animals are often unable to cross even moderately sized areas of unsuitable habitat.

Eighty percent of Massachusetts' turtles are listed as rare or endangered. The bog turtle shown above is on the endangered list.

Rare and Endangered Species

Seventy-three vertebrate animal species, or over 18% of Massachusetts' vertebrate wildlife, are presently listed by the Division of Fisheries and Wildlife as endangered, threatened or of special concern in the state. Fourteen percent of the Commonwealth's 1,700 native plant species are also classified into one of these three rare categories. The reason for this species population decline varies, but most frequently it is a result of habitat loss.

Of the several hundred state-listed rare species in Massachusetts, only 21 have been formally listed under the Federal Endangered Species Act; about half of them are marine species. The Natural Heritage and Endangered Species Program in the Division of Fisheries and Wildlife has, after ten years of field inventories, documented over 3,000 current occurrences of state-listed rare species. Although knowledge of the state's invertebrate fauna is incomplete, 89 species of invertebrates, primarily insects, have been listed as endangered, threatened or of special concern.

A majority of the species on both the state's rare plant and rare animal lists are wetland species. Although not all of the wetland species occur in riverine wetland habitats, rivers do provide critical habitat for many of the state's rare and endangered species. In addition to the eight species of state-listed rare fish (20% of the native inland fish), Massachusetts' rivers provide vital habitat for: globally endangered freshwater mussels, many rare dragonflies, endangered tiger beetles, Blanding's turtles, Britton's violet and river bulrush. State-threatened bird species such as the least bit-

tern, king rail, pied-billed grebe and the federally endangered bald eagle also inhabit river corridors in the state.

Some types of riverine habitats that the Commonwealth's rare species depend upon are: floodplain forests, river sandbars, claybanks, freshwater tidal marshes and extensive marshes dominated by emergent vegetation. Rare species are an important component of the Commonwealth's natural diversity. Protecting river corridors helps protect this natural heritage.

Endangered northern copperhead

Threatened least bittern —

Plants

2,700 Species recorded
(1,750* native and 950* introduced)
116 Native species considered endangered
80 Native species considered threatened
55 Native species considered special concern
50 Native species considered extirpated
or historical

*approximate

For a small state, Massachusetts is endowed with a relatively large and diverse flora because it is a crossroad for northern and southern plants. Over 1,750 species of native plants occur within its borders. Also occurring within the state are over 950 introduced or adventive species such as dandelion and purple loosestrife.

Geographic position, geology, and political boundaries all contribute to the diversity of Massachusetts' plants. Boston lies at a latitude where major weather patterns intersect and where cold and warm ocean currents meet. These factors play a major role in determining local climate and, in turn, where plants grow. Also, plants are often closely associated with specific bedrock or soil types, so that the state's complex geology is crucial to an understanding of plant distribution patterns. For example, the dolomite limestone of Berkshire County neutralizes acidity and provides minerals and nutrients essential to many plant species dependent upon them. It is no mere coincidence that nearly half of the state-listed rare plants in Massachusetts, with its mostly acidic substrate, occur in Berkshire County. Similarly, a large percentage of the state's rare plants occur in the limey, glacially-deposited sands of southeastern Massachusetts where warmer climatic conditions are comparable to those of more southerly regions. Boreal (northern) species seem quite at home on the Berkshire Plateau and in the Worcester County uplands where black spruce approaches its southern limit.

Rivers play a major role in shaping the landscape and creating habitat for flora and fauna. Major rivers such as the Housatonic and the Connecticut have meandered back and forth over time across their broad floodplains creating a variety of oxbow, pond, sandbar and floodplain forest habitats. Many of the state's plant species are associated with rivers, some of them exclusively so. Pin oak is found only in floodplain forests of immediate tributaries of the Connecticut River and occurs no further north in New England than Deerfield. Similarly, sandbar willow, a state-listed rare species, is found exclusively along the Connecticut's flood-scoured beaches. River birch, despite its wide range to the southwest of New England, is localized to the Merrimack and lower Concord rivers in the Commonwealth. Two herbaceous plants, narrow-leaved spring beauty and green dragon (both southerners and rare in the state), are found only in relatively undisturbed floodplain forests of the Connecticut, lower Deerfield and Housatonic rivers. Extensive clearing of these forests for their agriculturally superior soils has meant that the floodplain forest habitat and its unique species are now rare indeed. Finally, the hairy-fruited sedge is found solely in riverside marshes and swales of the Hoosic River, presumably having migrated from the Hudson River Valley of New York into Massachusetts.

Plymouth gentian (special concern)

Mountain laurel

Recreation

Americans prefer water-based forms of recreation more than any other type of leisure activity. With over 2,000 named rivers and streams in Massachusetts, residents and visitors alike are endowed with a variety of inexpensive and easily accessible river-based recreational opportunities.

Fishing

Fishing ranks as the second most popular recreational activity in the country. Over 240,000 licensed anglers and an estimated 150,000 unlicensed children fish in Massachusetts rivers and streams for over two dozen species of game fish and panfish.

The Division of Fisheries and Wildlife augments the wild fishery by stocking over 500,000 trout in 375 rivers and streams each year. The division also stocks northern pike, tiger muskie and land-locked salmon. Restoration of Atlantic salmon and American shad in the Merrimack and Connecticut rivers is underway as well.

Anglers at Jamaica Pond

CURRENT FRESHWATER SPORTFISHING RECORDS		
GAME SPECIES		
Brook Trout	6 lbs. 4 oz.	1968
*Brown Trout	19 lbs. 10 oz.	1966
*Lake Trout	22 lbs. 10 oz.	1988
*Rainbow Trout	13 lbs. 0 oz.	1984
*LL Salmon	10 lbs. 2 oz.	1985
*Largemouth	15 lbs. 8 oz.	1975
*Smallmouth	7 lbs. 4 oz.	1984
*Walleye	11 lbs. 0 oz.	1975
Ch. Pickerel	9 lbs. 5 oz.	1954
*Northern Pike	35 lbs. 0 oz.	1988
American Shad	11 lbs. 4 oz.	1986
*Channel Cat	26 lbs. 8 oz.	1989
*White Cat	9 lbs. 3 oz.	1987
*Carp	42 lbs. 8 oz.	1988
*Tiger Muskie	19 lbs. 4 oz.	1987
PAN SPECIES		
Yellow Perch	2 lbs. 12 oz.	1979
White Perch	2 lbs. 15 oz.	1988 & 1989
*Crappie/Calico	4 lbs. 10 oz.	1980
Bullhead	3 lbs. 8 oz.	1985 & 1987
Sunfish	2 lbs. 1 oz.	1982

*Introduced species
Note: Sunfish includes bluegills, an introduced species, and pumpkinseeds which are native to Massachusetts. Bullheads include both brown and yellow bullhead.

A boy's first shad

Canoeing

The Appalachian Mountain Club has classified almost 700 river miles on 58 rivers in Massachusetts as suitable for family-type flat water canoeing. Another 340 miles have been designated suitable for white water enthusiasts.

A canoeing experience on the Nashua River

Other River Related Recreation

River and river corridor lands are popular for a number of other recreational pursuits, including swimming, boating, hiking, camping, hunting, cross-country skiing and bird watching.

Urban rivers, such as the Charles, provide a scenic backdrop for thousands of people who bicycle, jog or walk on paths along the river's banks. Many Heritage State Parks focus on the importance of rivers to the state's cities. Among other things, the parks explain the vital role that rivers have played and continue to play in the industrial development and culture of many of Massachusetts' cities.

A successful deer hunting trip

Clearly, an ecologically sound policy of river corridor protection not only provides ecological and socioeconomic benefits; it also goes a long way in providing easily accessible, inexpensive, localized forms of recreation popular among Massachusetts' residents and visitors to the state.

Sculling on the Charles River

The old swimming hole

Socioeconomic Values
of River Corridor Protection

"Investment in environmental protection is good economic policy."

Governor Michael S. Dukakis
1987

All the previously mentioned environmental and recreational values of protected river corridors have direct and indirect economic translations.

Direct Economic Returns

The U.S. Fish and Wildlife Service and the U.S. Census Bureau estimate that recreational anglers spend $492 million every year in Massachusetts on fishing trips, licensing and gear. This results in over $21 million in direct tax revenue to the state. Of this total, about 90% is related to marine fishing and 10% to freshwater recreational fishing.

Pike fishing

Massachusetts' marine commercial fishery ranks third in the nation in net off-vessel value—over $300 million in 1988. Processing and retailing of this resource generates over $1.5 billion in economic activity and provides 15,000 jobs. Nearly 70% of Massachusetts' marine fin and shellfish depend on estuaries at the mouths of freshwater rivers for important parts of their lifecycles; clearly, there are critical economic reasons for keeping Massachusetts' rivers and their estuaries protected and healthy.

Scituate Harbor commercial fishing fleet

Other outdoor activities such as canoeing, cross country skiing, nature observation, photography and numerous other natural forms of outdoor recreation generate jobs, economic activity and tax revenue to the state. For example, a 1985 U.S. Fish and Wildlife survey estimates that residents of Massachusetts spend an astounding $71 million on bird-related books, equipment, nesting boxes and birdseed each year.

The economic value of open space to the Massachusetts' economy, according to 1985 figures, is estimated at almost $3 billion. Tourism, agriculture, hunting, fishing and forestry are key contributors to this figure. In addition, wetlands, watersheds and aquifer recharge areas provide flood protection and assure water quality and supply.

Less Direct Economic Returns

Wetlands are one of the most important habitats for fish and wildlife; they are also a major component of riparian corridors. In 1985, the U.S. Department of the Interior calculated that it would cost $85,000 to restore or replicate an acre of wetland.

Wetlands of the Westboro Wildlife Management Area

The public has invested $2.4 billion to abate pollution in Massachusetts' rivers since passage of the 1972 Clean Water Act. Now, a much smaller investment in river corridor protection would help prevent additional pollution and guarantee public access to that investment. Also, protected river corridors would link many existing open spaces and thus protect and enhance yet another multimillion dollar public investment. Nowhere is the adage "an ounce of prevention is worth a pound of cure" more applicable than to investments in riparian corridor protection.

Wastewater treatment plant on the Nashua River in Clinton is being updated and scheduled for completion in 1993.

Indirect Economic Returns

Massachusetts' rich historic and cultural heritage is inextricably linked to rivers. Rivers and streams influenced the location of early native American villages that are of historic and archaeological interest today. More recently, Massachusetts' rivers spawned the American Industrial Revolution. The Blackstone River and its associated canal system is one of only two interstate (Massachusetts / Rhode Island) industrial rivers affiliated with the national park system because of its contribution to early industrial growth. Lowell, Lawrence, Leominster, Northampton, Holyoke, Springfield, Blackstone, Taunton and many other industrial cities in Massachusetts owe their existence and prosperity to rivers.

Early industry relied on water power. Pictured above is the old grist mill in Sudbury.

In later years, when many of these old industrial centers fell on economic hard times, the rivers came to the rescue. Rivers such as the Merrimack in Lowell often provide a catalyst and a theme for public and private reinvestment and eventual economic revitalization for declining old milltown economies (see Section V on the Nashua River for a description of how a relatively small stream is drawing private investment in the city of Leominster). Individual private businesses and commercial and residential developers are finding that it is directly profitable to contribute funding, open land and other assistance to river corridor protection.

Another important aspect of the value of healthy rivers concerns protection of our water supplies. Sixty-six percent of the state's population relies on surface water for water supply sources, either from rivers directly or from reservoirs, almost all of which are fed by streams. The cost of filtering and treating drinking water is astronomical. For example, the Massachusetts Water Resources Authority (MWRA) has estimated the cost of building a water treatment plant for the Quabbin Reservoir, if it becomes necessary, at $300 to $500 million—and this price does not even include operational costs. Preservation of watershed land is almost always more effective and less expensive in safeguarding water supplies.

Fun on a summer's day

However, the most important valuation of our natural systems, including our rivers, probably cannot be expressed in financial terms. Nearly everyone has a river in their lives—whether from childhood, near home or as a favorite recreational hideaway. There is no price that can be placed upon the quality of life or the character of our cities and towns, which is shaped by our natural systems and often highlighted by our rivers.

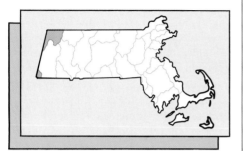

River Basin: Hoosic, Kinderhook, Bashbish

Total Drainage Area:
 Hoosic Basin: 12,650 sq. mi.
 Kinderhook Basin: 329 sq. mi.
 Bashbish Basin: 16 sq. mi.
Drainage Area in MA:
 Hoosic Basin: 203 sq. mi.
 Kinderhook Basin: 21.9 sq. mi.
 Bashbish Basin: 15.5 sq. mi.
Source of River:
 Hoosic: Above Cheshire Reservoir
 Kinderhook: Brooks in Hancock
 Bashbish: Brooks in
 Mt. Washington
Mouth of River: Hudson River
Total River Length: Hoosic: 57.3 mi.
River Length in MA:
 Hoosic: 20.9 mi.
 Kinderhook: 4.8 mi.
 Bashbish: 2.0 mi.
Major Tributaries: Green River
Acres of Ponds, Lakes, Reservoirs:
 Hoosic Basin: 624
 Kinderhook Basin: 28
 Bashbish Basin: 41
Wastewater Discharges:
 Municipal Treatment Plants 2
 Other 2
Features: Mt. Greylock, Mt. Greylock State Reservation, Mt. Greylock War Memorial, Appalachian Trail, Taconic Trail, Bashbish Falls, Clarksburg State Park, Berry Pond (highest pond in Massachusetts)

Hoosic, Kinderhook & Bashbish River Basins

Unlike most other Massachusetts' rivers, the Hoosic flows north and west, thus serving as a corridor into Massachusetts for animals and birds normally associated with regions further north. In addition, the soils are influenced by limestone rocks which buffer the normally acidic soil conditions in the state. These unique soils, in combination with a mountainous terrain, high altitude and consequent variations in temperature and precipitation, contribute to a variety of plant species which are not found in other areas of the state.

This region is the only area in Massachusetts with a truly alpine character. The best spruce-fir forest in the state is found on Mount Greylock, the state's highest point at 3,491 feet. The basin also has some undisturbed old growth forest.

Although PCBs (poly-chlorinated biphenyls) pose a pollution problem on the main stem of the river, the Division of Fisheries and Wildlife presently augments wild trout populations with stocked trout for "catch and release" fishing. Tributaries such as the south branch and the Green River are premier cold water trout streams, and ponds such as Cheshire Lake produce an abundance of species, including northern pike.

From its headwaters above Cheshire Reservoir, the Hoosic is known as "the invisible river" because it is hidden behind hedgerows and meanders quietly through farmlands in this flat section of the basin. In Adams and North Adams, the river was severely channeled by the Army Corps of Engineers after serious flooding took place in the 1930's; here it runs through concrete beds and banks. As it turns northwest and passes beyond Williamstown, the river becomes a cobble-bottomed beauty, regaining its earlier form and character—a canoeist's treasure. New treatment plants and the concern of a strong and relatively new watershed association have begun to make a measurable difference in the river's present condition and its future.

Like the Hoosic, both the Kinderhook and Bashbish rivers are tributaries of the Hudson River, although these rivers flow to the southwest. Both the Kinderhook and the Bashbish watersheds are characterized by rugged landscapes typical of the Massachusetts-New York border region.

Rare Species:

Plants: northern mountain ash, northern bog violet, Braun's holly fern ●, ginseng, bristly black current
Animals: blackpoll warbler, American bald eagle #

● Endangered in Massachusetts
Federally Endangered

Bashbish Falls

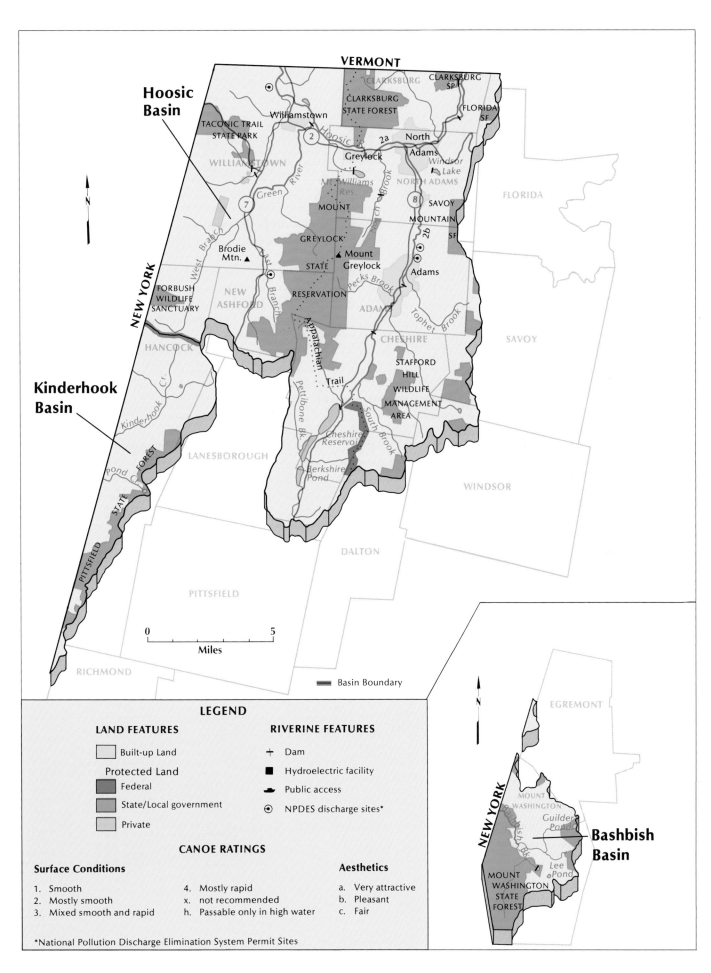

VERMONT

Hoosic Basin

CLARKSBURG
CLARKSBURG SP
CLARKSBURG STATE FOREST
FLORIDA SF

Williamstown

TACONIC TRAIL STATE PARK

Hoosic R.

2a

North Adams

Greylock

WILLIAMSTOWN

Windsor Lake

NORTH ADAMS

FLORIDA

Green River

Mt. Williams Res.

MOUNT

SAVOY MOUNTAIN

8

2b

SF

West Branch

Brodie Mtn. ▲

GREYLOCK

▲ Mount Greylock

FORBUSH WILDLIFE SANCTUARY

NEW YORK

NEW ASHFORD

STATE

Pecks Brook

Adams

RESERVATION

ADAMS

HANCOCK

Cass Branch

Pettibone Bk.

Appalachian

Tophet Brook

CHESHIRE

SAVOY

Kinderhook Basin

Kinderhook Cr.

Trail

STAFFORD HILL WILDLIFE MANAGEMENT AREA

South Brook

FOREST

LANESBOROUGH

Cheshire Reservoir

WINDSOR

Pond Cr.

PITTSFIELD STATE

Berkshire Pond

DALTON

PITTSFIELD

0   5
Miles

RICHMOND

▬▬ Basin Boundary

LEGEND

LAND FEATURES

☐ Built-up Land

Protected Land

■ Federal

■ State/Local government

■ Private

RIVERINE FEATURES

+ Dam

■ Hydroelectric facility

⌐ Public access

⊙ NPDES discharge sites*

CANOE RATINGS

Surface Conditions

1. Smooth
2. Mostly smooth
3. Mixed smooth and rapid

4. Mostly rapid
x. not recommended
h. Passable only in high water

Aesthetics

a. Very attractive
b. Pleasant
c. Fair

*National Pollution Discharge Elimination System Permit Sites

EGREMONT

NEW YORK

MOUNT WASHINGTON

Guilder Pond

Bashbish Basin

Bashbish Bk.

Lee Pond

MOUNT WASHINGTON STATE FOREST

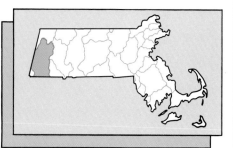

River Basin: Housatonic

Total Drainage Area: 1,950 sq. mi.
Drainage Area in MA: 500 sq. mi.
Source of River: 3 lakes near Pittsfield
Mouth of River: Long Island Sound
Total River Length: 150.9 mi.
River Length in MA: 66.5 mi.
Major Tributaries: Green River, Williams River, East Branch
Acres of Ponds, Lakes, Reservoirs: 5,184
Hydropower Facilities: 3; 565 kw
Wastewater Discharges:
Municipal Treatment Plants 6
Other 8
Features: Appalachian Trail, Housatonic River Valley Wildlife Management Area, Bartholomew's Cobble, Beartown State Forest, Waconah Falls State Park, Hinsdale Flats Wildlife Management Area, Monument Mountain

Rare Species:

Plants: showy lady's-slipper, swamp birch, hemlock parsley, purple cliff brake, purple cress ●, deocious sedge
Animals: bog turtle ●, northern spring salamander

● Endangered in Massachusetts

Housatonic River Basin

The Housatonic River, whose name among the Mahican Indians meant "the place beyond the mountains," rises out of three ponds, the largest of which is Onota Lake in Pittsfield. The river begins as fast-flowing streams that unite in the Berkshire Valley. From there it meanders through extensive floodplains, passes through Connecticut, and empties into the ocean at Long Island Sound.

The Housatonic drainage offers exceptional fishing opportunities. Thirty pound, forty inch northern pike have been caught in Onota Lake, and 3-foot long tiger muskie are routinely caught in Pontoosuc Lake. Although there is an advisory against eating fish caught out of the river's main stem below Pittsfield because of PCB contamination, the river is an excellent "catch and release" recreational fishery. Pristine tributaries, such as the southwest branch, support wild populations of brook and brown trout. The Housatonic and its tributaries also offer a variety of canoeing options, ranging from difficult and sometimes dangerous patches of rapids sought out by white water enthusiasts, to leisurely stretches suitable for a family canoe trip.

The combination of abundant marble outcrops (which neutralize the generally acidic soils in the watershed) and the pronounced meandering path of the river along the flat valley floor makes the basin one of the most biologically diverse regions of the state—second only to Cape Cod in the large number of rare and endangered species. The bog turtle is found only in this watershed in Massachusetts. Numerous adjacent marshes and oxbows provide exceptional stopover and nesting areas for Canadian geese, black and wood duck and many other waterfowl species. Deer, bear, upland game and non-game wildlife abound throughout the basin.

Housatonic River, Sheffield

Rare at one time, beaver now flourish in the Housatonic Basin and throughout most of the state.

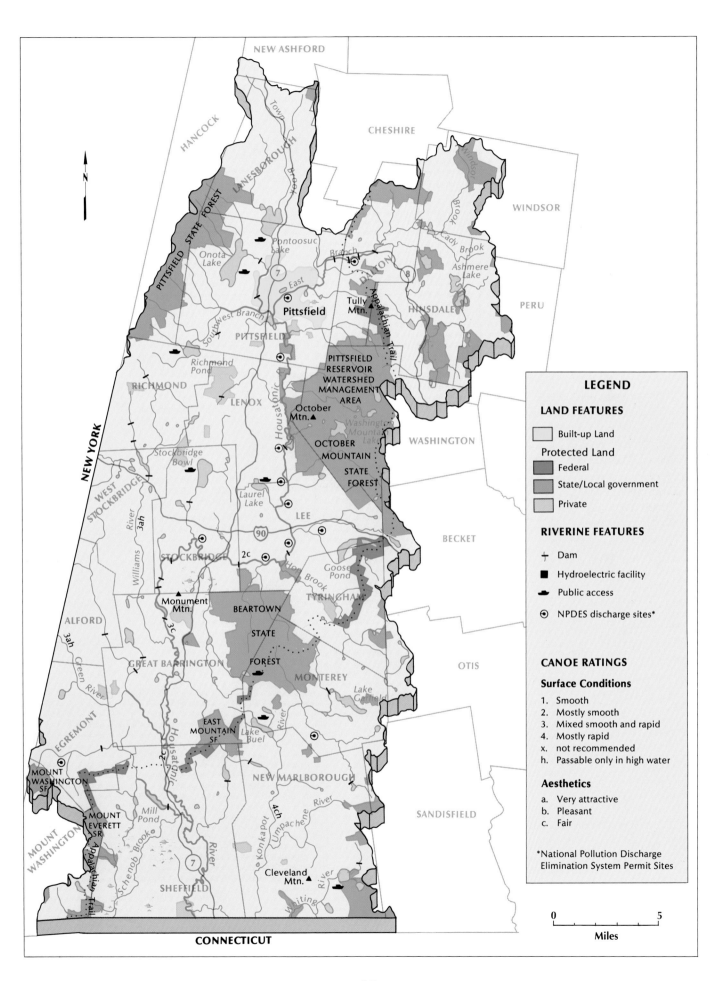

LEGEND

LAND FEATURES

Built-up Land

Protected Land

Federal

State/Local government

Private

RIVERINE FEATURES

✛ Dam

■ Hydroelectric facility

🛶 Public access

⊙ NPDES discharge sites*

CANOE RATINGS

Surface Conditions

1. Smooth
2. Mostly smooth
3. Mixed smooth and rapid
4. Mostly rapid
x. not recommended
h. Passable only in high water

Aesthetics

a. Very attractive
b. Pleasant
c. Fair

*National Pollution Discharge
Elimination System Permit Sites

0 ————— 5
Miles

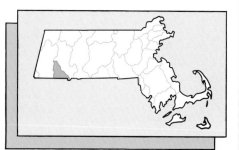

River Basin:
Farmington

Total Drainage Area: 602 sq. mi.
Drainage Area in MA: 100 sq. mi.
Source of River: brooks in Becket
Mouth of River: Connecticut River
Total River Length: 78.4 mi.
River Length in MA: 18 mi.
Acres of Ponds, Lakes, Reservoirs: 3,583
Hydropower Facilities: 0
Features: Sandisfield State Forest, Otis Reservoir, Tolland State Forest

Rare Species:

Plants: arethusa and dwarf mistletoe
Animals: northern spring salamander

Farmington River Basin

The headwaters of the Farmington River lie in Massachusetts, but more than three-quarters of this basin (which drains into the Connecticut River) lies in the state of Connecticut. The Massachusetts portion of the basin is hilly with many small feeder streams originating on steep slopes. The river is characterized by numerous rapids created by an average fall rate of about 100 feet per mile. Long protected by Connecticut's Metropolitan District Water Bureau (which owns major portions of the basin even in Massachusetts), the river is still relatively pure and free flowing. Several state parks within the basin make it a popular area for fishing, hunting, camping, canoeing and hiking.

The soils and forests of the Farmington are typical of Massachusetts and similar to the adjacent Westfield Basin; the northern spring salamander is one of only a few rare species that live in the Massachusetts portion of the basin.

Fall River in Otis

Northern spring salamander

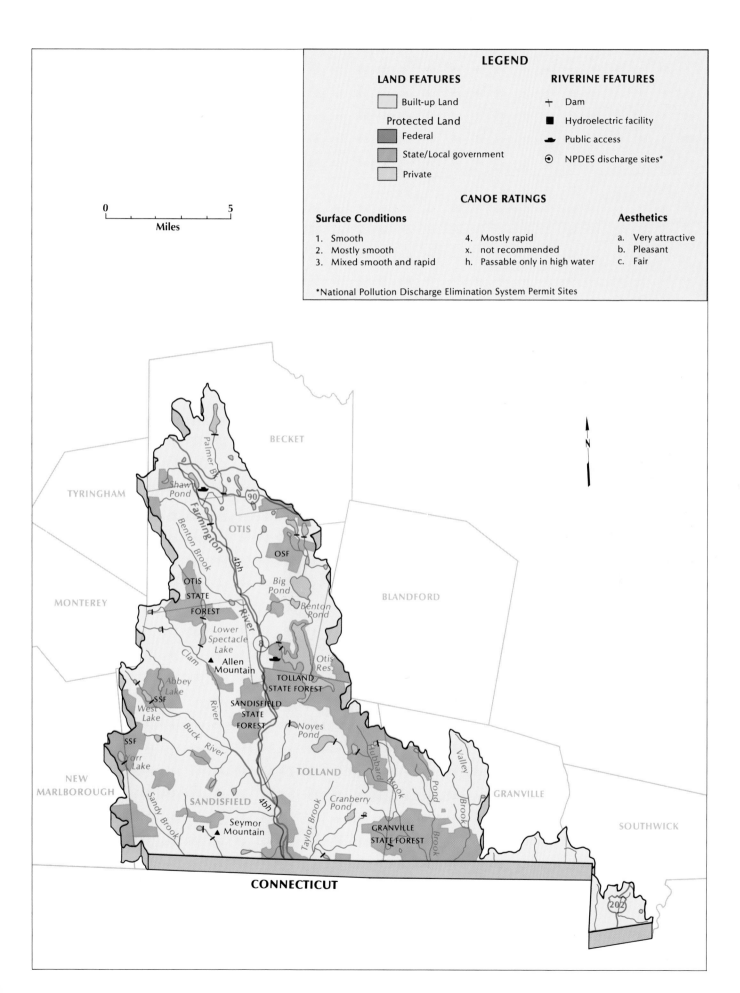

LEGEND

LAND FEATURES

Built-up Land

Protected Land
Federal

State/Local government

Private

RIVERINE FEATURES

+ Dam

■ Hydroelectric facility

Public access

⊙ NPDES discharge sites*

CANOE RATINGS

Surface Conditions

1. Smooth
2. Mostly smooth
3. Mixed smooth and rapid

4. Mostly rapid
x. not recommended
h. Passable only in high water

Aesthetics

a. Very attractive
b. Pleasant
c. Fair

*National Pollution Discharge Elimination System Permit Sites

0 ——— 5
Miles

BECKET

TYRINGHAM

OTIS

OSF

OTIS STATE FOREST

Palmer Bk.

Shaw Pond

Farmington River

Benton Brook

Big Pond

Benton Pond

BLANDFORD

MONTEREY

Lower Spectacle Lake

Allen Mountain

Clam

TOLLAND STATE FOREST

Otis Res.

Abbey Lake

SSF

West Lake

SANDISFIELD STATE FOREST

River

Buck River

Noyes Pond

SSF

Dorr Lake

Hubbard Brook

Pond

Valley Brook

GRANVILLE

NEW MARLBOROUGH

Sandy Brook

SANDISFIELD

TOLLAND

Taylor Brook

Cranberry Pond

GRANVILLE STATE FOREST

Brook

Seymor Mountain

SOUTHWICK

CONNECTICUT

202

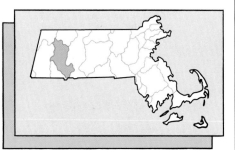

River Basin: Westfield

Total Drainage Area: 517 sq. mi.
Drainage Area in MA: 517 sq. mi.
Source of River: brooks on eastern side of southern Berkshires in Savoy
Mouth of River: Connecticut River
River Length in MA: 27 mi.
Major Tributaries: Swift River, Middle Branch, Little River, West Branch
Acres of Lakes, Ponds, Reservoirs: 4,551
Hydropower Facilities: 5; 39,690 kw
Wastewater Discharges: Municipal Treatment Plants 3 Other 3
Features: Chesterfield Gorge

Rare Species:

Plants: spurred gentian, narrow-leaved spring beauty, large-leaved sandwort
Animals: Jefferson salamander, American bittern, eastern small-footed bat, lake chub ●

●   Endangered in Massachusetts

Westfield River Basin

The Westfield River system illustrates the remarkable geographic contrast that makes Massachusetts so unique. While the upper reaches of its three main branches emanate from steep forested hills and wooded valleys, the lower sections of the main stem flow through flat farmland and increasingly urban areas.

The Westfield's long east branch offers the most diverse canoeing, from very difficult rapids to placid waters suitable for the novice. This branch descends over 1,000 feet in its first fourteen miles. One notable feature on the east branch, the Chesterfield Gorge, is a spectacular scenic area—a box canyon between sheer granite cliffs topped by tall hemlocks and spruce. The Middle and West branches of the Westfield are slightly smaller than the east branch. They flow through picturesque valleys and their crystal clear waters offer excellent fishing.

Native trout populations are present in parts of the main stem, the Middle Branch and the Littleville Reservoir. In April of 1989, thousands of salmon par and fry were stocked in the Westfield as part of the effort to restore Atlantic salmon which have not lived in the basin for over 200 years.

The soils and vegetation of the basin, and thus the wildlife species, are fairly typical of the state. Deer, bear, wild turkey and bobcat are all present in the watershed. There are also some notable rare species, such as the threatened lake chub, found only in this basin in Massachusetts.

Black bear cub

Westfield River south of Chesterfield Gorge

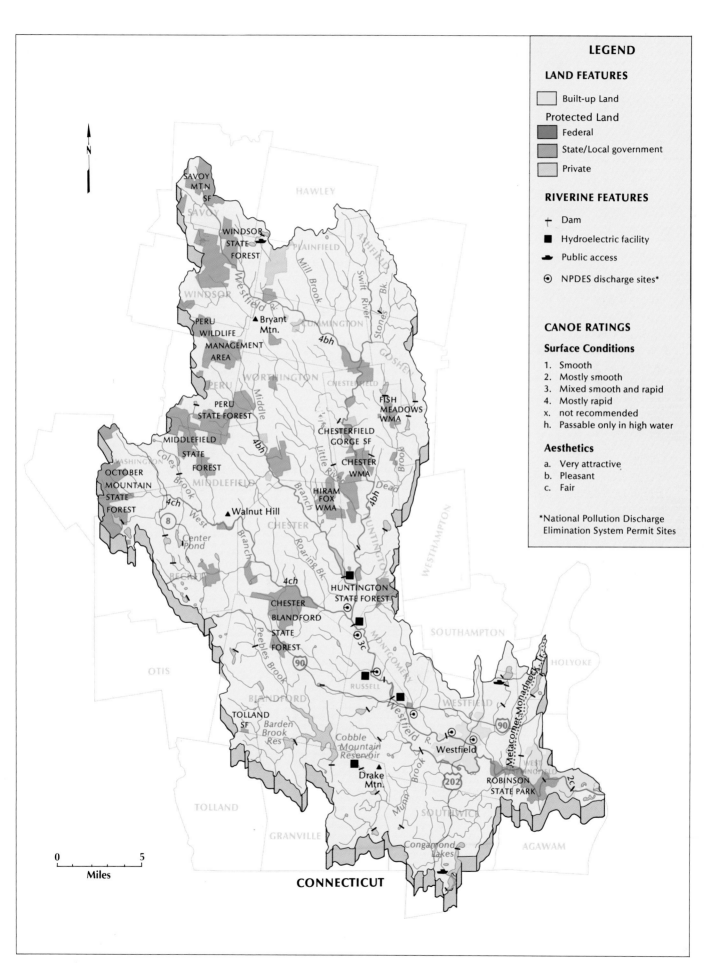

LEGEND

LAND FEATURES

Built-up Land

Protected Land

Federal

State/Local government

Private

RIVERINE FEATURES

† Dam

■ Hydroelectric facility

➤ Public access

⊙ NPDES discharge sites*

CANOE RATINGS

Surface Conditions

1. Smooth
2. Mostly smooth
3. Mixed smooth and rapid
4. Mostly rapid
x. not recommended
h. Passable only in high water

Aesthetics

a. Very attractive
b. Pleasant
c. Fair

*National Pollution Discharge
Elimination System Permit Sites

SAVOY MT N SF

SAVOY

WINDSOR STATE FOREST

HAWLEY

PLAINFIELD

WINDSOR

Mill Brook

ASHFIELD

Swift River

Stones Bk.

PERU WILDLIFE MANAGEMENT AREA

▲ Bryant Mtn.

HUNTINGTON

4bh

Westfield R.

GOSHEN

PERU

WORTHINGTON

Middle

CHESTERFIELD

PERU STATE FOREST

4bh

Little River

FISH MEADOWS WMA

MIDDLEFIELD STATE FOREST

CHESTERFIELD GORGE SF

Coles Brook

MIDDLEFIELD

Branch

CHESTER WMA

Brook

OCTOBER MOUNTAIN STATE FOREST

WASHINGTON

HIRAM FOX WMA

Dead

4ch

West Branch

▲ Walnut Hill

CHESTER

8

Roaring Bk.

4bh

HUNTINGTON

WESTHAMPTON

Center Pond

Branch

4ch

HUNTINGTON STATE FOREST

⊙

BECKET

CHESTER BLANDFORD STATE FOREST

3c ⊙

MONTGOMERY

SOUTHAMPTON

Metacomet-Monadnock Tr.

HOLYOKE

90

RUSSELL

■

WESTFIELD

90

TOLLAND SF

Peebles Brook

OTIS

Barden Brook Res

BLANDFORD

Westfield R.

⊙

⊙

Cobble Mountain Reservoir

Westfield

202

WEST SPRINGFIELD

2c

OTIS

Drake Mtn. ▲

Munn Brook

ROBINSON STATE PARK

TOLLAND

SOUTHWICK

AGAWAM

GRANVILLE

Congamond Lakes

➤

CONNECTICUT

0   5

Miles

N

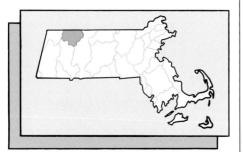

River Basin: Deerfield

Total Drainage Area: 665 sq. mi.
Drainage Area in MA: 350 sq. mi.
Source of River: Vermont
Mouth of River: Connecticut River
Total River Length: 70.2 mi.
River Length in MA: 39.0 mi.
Major Tributaries: North River, Green River, Chickley River, Cold River
Acres of Ponds, Lakes, Reservoirs: 589
Hydropower Facilities: 8; 653,980 kw
Wastewater Discharges: Municipal Treatment Plants 6 Other 1
Features: Hoosic Tunnel, Mohawk Trail State Forest, Bridge of Flowers at Shelburne Falls, Yankee Atomic Plant at Rowe

Rare Species:

Plants: black maple, mountain alder, ginseng, nodding pogonia ●, showy lady's-slipper, Michaux's sedge ●
Animals: northern spring salamander

● Endangered in Massachusetts

Deerfield River Basin

In the 1880's, rainbow trout eggs from the McCloud River in California were shipped across the country via railroad car and transplanted into the Deerfield River. Today, a century later, this strain of trout no longer lives in the McCloud River, but it is thriving in the pristine waters of the Deerfield Basin.

The Deerfield is one of the cleanest and coldest rivers in the state. Its tributaries support more naturally reproducing populations of rainbow trout than any other drainage and the basin's rugged forests also host the Commonwealth's densest black bear population.

The watershed includes some stands of old growth hardwood-conifer forests on slopes considered too steep to log. Stands of red spruce, yellow birch and sugar maple, with trees well over 100 feet, receive protection in several state forests and provide habitat for many upland wildlife species.

The Deerfield watershed has unusually cool and moist climatic conditions, including the highest average precipitation in the state at 50 inches annually. Due to their high elevation, the slopes of the Berkshire Plateau receive more snow, and hold it longer, than most other parts of the state. Cool temperatures slow the decomposition of organic matter and help to maintain peat in bogs and fens. This creates an area rich in unusual mosses, whose nearest relatives are found in Nova Scotia.

The pristine waters, relatively undisturbed forests, wildlife and scenic vistas of the mountains and Deerfield Valley attract many hikers and campers to the region. There are several superb hiking trails both adjacent to the river and in upland forests. Excellent white water stretches on the main stem and tributaries are used year-round by recreational canoeists and kayakers, and a slalom kayak course at Zoar Gapp in Charlemont is used by world-class kayakers as a training site for Olympic white water kayak racing.

Deerfield River in Conway

Lower Deerfield River

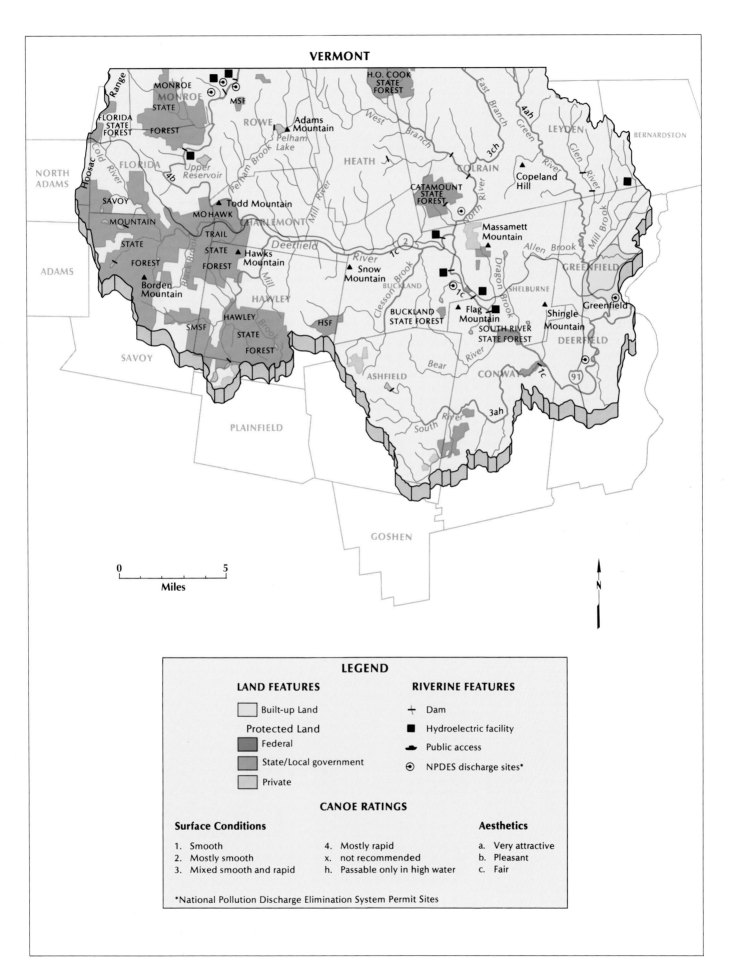

VERMONT

LEGEND

LAND FEATURES

Built-up Land

Protected Land

Federal

State/Local government

Private

RIVERINE FEATURES

+ Dam

■ Hydroelectric facility

Public access

⊙ NPDES discharge sites*

CANOE RATINGS

Surface Conditions

1. Smooth
2. Mostly smooth
3. Mixed smooth and rapid
4. Mostly rapid
x. not recommended
h. Passable only in high water

Aesthetics

a. Very attractive
b. Pleasant
c. Fair

*National Pollution Discharge Elimination System Permit Sites

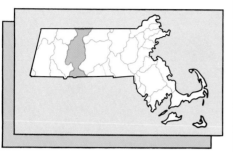

River Basin: Connecticut

Total Drainage Area: 11,250 sq. mi.

Drainage Area in MA: 660 sq. mi.

Source of River: Near Canadian Border

Mouth of River: Long Island Sound

Total River Length: 409 mi.

River Length in MA: 66 mi.

Major Tributaries: Millers River, Deerfield River, Chicopee River, Westfield River

Acres of Ponds, Lakes, Reservoirs: 2,933

Wastewater Discharges: Municipal Treatment Plants 10 Other 70

Hydropower Facilities: 25; 953,122 kw

Features: Oxbow Lake, Holyoke Mountain Range, Northfield Mountain Pump Station, Sunderland Fish Hatchery, Holyoke Heritage State Park, Holyoke fish ladders, Mount Sugarloaf, French King Bridge

Rare Species:

Plants: sandbar willow, purple clematis, green dragon, putty root ●, ram's head lady's-slipper ●, cattail sedge, climbing fern

Animals: short-nosed sturgeon ●, Jefferson salamander, grasshopper sparrows, upland sandpiper ●, American bald eagle #

●   Endangered in Massachusetts

Federally Endangered

Connecticut River Basin

The mighty Connecticut River is the largest river in Massachusetts. It originates near the Canadian border, acts as the boundary between Vermont and New Hampshire, and enters Massachusetts in Northfield. It flows 66 miles south into Connecticut, eventually draining into Long Island Sound. The dam at Holyoke divides the Massachusetts portion of the river into two distinct segments. The northern segment runs through primarily rural and agricultural areas which have recently been impacted by housing developments. The southern portion runs through land that was intensely developed for industry long ago.

The flat floodplains of the Connecticut Valley are some of the state's most productive farmlands. Several town names in the area contain the word-ending "field." Many diverse geological characteristics provide habitat that attract species not found elsewhere in the state. Channel changes over the years have left oxbows in the river's former course. The largest oxbow lake in the state is located in Northampton. Some islands in the river retain rare prairie-like grasslands. Only the Housatonic Basin and the Cape Cod Basin have more rare species than the Connecticut River Basin.

Waterfowl migrating along the Atlantic flyway use the river as an important resting and feeding area. The endangered American bald eagle and the once threatened osprey are frequently sighted along the river corridor. The river supports many fish species including trophy-sized northern pike, large and smallmouth bass and the endangered short-nosed sturgeon. Over $60 million have been spent on the construction of fish lifts and fish ladders in successful efforts to restore spring runs of American shad. The Atlantic salmon may one day follow. The world record American shad was caught in the Connecticut River in 1986.

The river also provides an abundance of opportunities for camping, boating and other outdoor activities. Faced with the acceleration of development in the Connecticut Valley, both state and local governments have initiated major programs aimed at the preservation of some of the state's most beautiful and fertile farmlands, lush forest habitats and quaint river villages.

Aerial view of the Connecticut River

Shad fishing on the Connecticut River

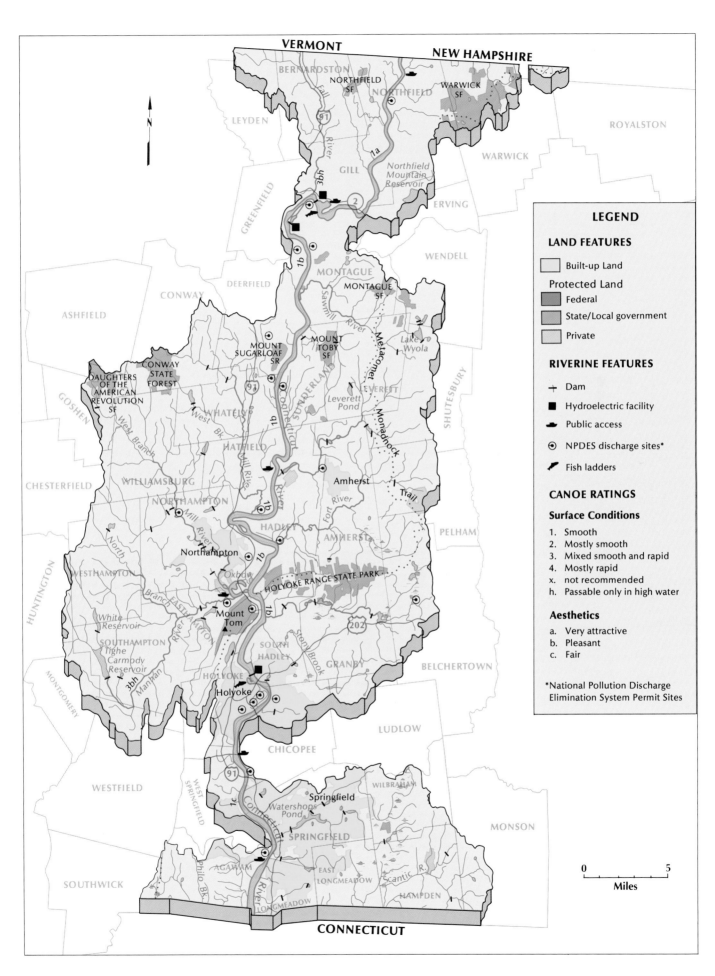

VERMONT **NEW HAMPSHIRE**

BERNARDSTON

NORTHFIELD SF

NORTHFIELD

WARWICK SF

LEYDEN

ROYALSTON

WARWICK

GILL

Northfield Mountain Reservoir

ERVING

GREENFIELD

WENDELL

MONTAGUE

DEERFIELD

CONWAY

MONTAGUE SF

Sawmill River

ASHFIELD

MOUNT SUGARLOAF SR

MOUNT TOBY SF

Lake Wyola

CONWAY STATE FOREST

Metacomet

DAUGHTERS OF THE AMERICAN REVOLUTION SF

SUNDERLAND

LEVERETT

SHUTESBURY

WHATELY

Leverett Pond

GOSHEN

West Bk.

Monadnock

HATFIELD

Mill River

Amherst

Trail

CHESTERFIELD

WILLIAMSBURG

Fort River

NORTHAMPTON

PELHAM

Mill River

AMHERST

HADLEY

Northampton

North

Oxbow

HOLYOKE RANGE STATE PARK

WESTHAMPTON

Branch EAST

Mount Tom

Stony Brook

SOUTH HADLEY

HUNTINGTON

White Reservoir

GRANBY

BELCHERTOWN

SOUTHAMPTON

Tighe Carmody Reservoir

HOLYOKE

MONTGOMERY

Manhan

Holyoke

LUDLOW

WESTFIELD

WEST SPRINGFIELD

CHICOPEE

WILBRAHAM

Springfield

Watershops Pond

MONSON

SPRINGFIELD

Connecticut

Scantic R.

SOUTHWICK

Philo Bk.

AGAWAM

EAST LONGMEADOW

Connecticut River

LONGMEADOW

HAMPDEN

CONNECTICUT

43

LEGEND

LAND FEATURES

Built-up Land

Protected Land

Federal

State/Local government

Private

RIVERINE FEATURES

⊢ Dam

■ Hydroelectric facility

Public access

⊙ NPDES discharge sites*

Fish ladders

CANOE RATINGS

Surface Conditions

1. Smooth
2. Mostly smooth
3. Mixed smooth and rapid
4. Mostly rapid
x. not recommended
h. Passable only in high water

Aesthetics

a. Very attractive
b. Pleasant
c. Fair

*National Pollution Discharge Elimination System Permit Sites

0   5
Miles

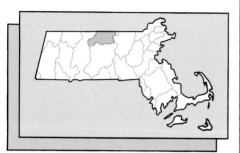

River Basin:
Millers

Total Drainage Area: 392 sq. mi.

Drainage Area in MA: 320 sq. mi.

Source of River: NH and
North Central MA

Mouth of River: Connecticut
River

Total River Length: 51 mi.

River Length in MA: 43.8 mi.

Major Tributaries: Otter River,
Tully River

Acres of Ponds, Lakes, Reservoirs:
3,540

Hydropower Facilities:
6; 797 kw

Wastewater Discharges:
Municipal Treatment Plants 8
Other 5

Features: Erving State Forest,
Millers River Wildlife Manage-
ment Area, Mount Grace State
Forest, Lake Dennison State Park,
Birch Hill Dam, Tully Lake

Rare Species:

Plants: Bartram's shadbush,
dwarf mistletoe, sand violet ●

● Endangered in Massachusetts

Millers River Basin

From its origins in New Hampshire and North Central Massachusetts, the Millers River flows south and then gradually moves west. The watershed of the Millers is hilly with uplands ranging from 200 to 1,500 feet in altitude. The basin's soils and vegetation are characteristic of the rest of the state. The glacial till (rubble left by the glacial retreat) is quite acidic and cannot buffer the effects of acid rain in the basin, thus leaving the river and its aquatic life vulnerable to damage. Most of the forests are young second growth areas of a pine-oak mix.

Originally, the waters of the Millers River were full of salmon, trout and other fish. Settlement in the seventeenth century ushered in dams and mills which began to change the character and quality of the water. In the 1930's and 1940's the river was still one of the best stocked trout streams in the state. However, by the 1950's pollution from industrial and domestic sources had ruined the Millers for fishing and recreation. The river's color would vary from day to day, depending on what dyes the paper mills upstream were discharging. After a long period of neglect, the local watershed council began the arduous task of orchestrating a cleanup. Within ten years, by 1983, the river was clean enough to stock again. Unfortunately, a high concentration of PCBs (poly-chlorinated biphenyls) were detected in fish. As a result, a section of the river is currently designated for "catch and release" fishing only.

The annual River Rat Race on the Millers River

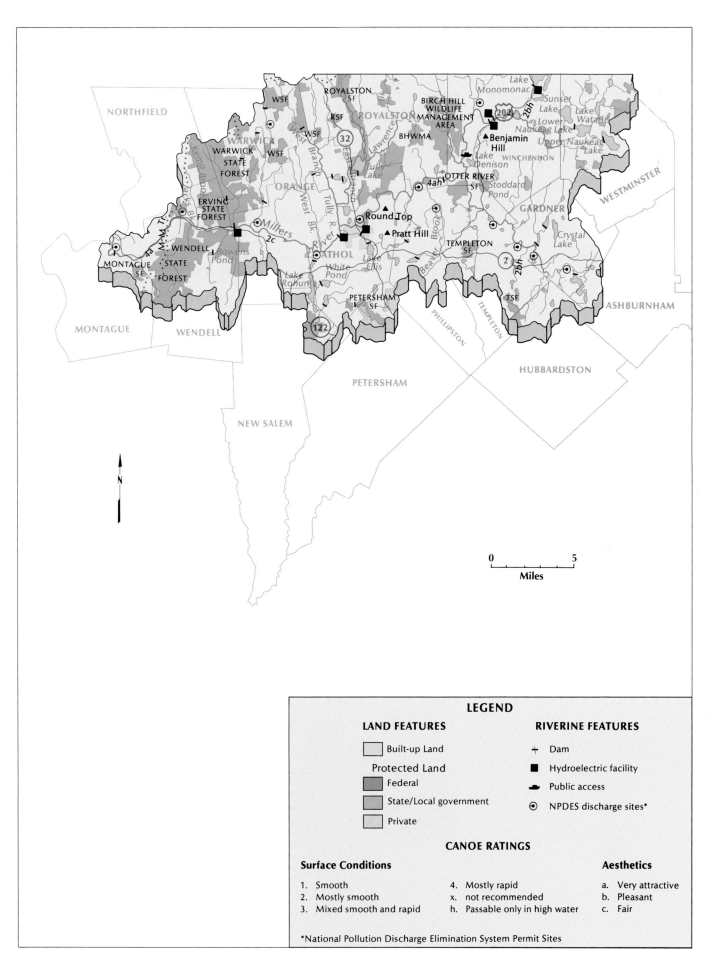

LEGEND

LAND FEATURES

Built-up Land

Protected Land

Federal

State/Local government

Private

RIVERINE FEATURES

✛ Dam

■ Hydroelectric facility

⚓ Public access

⊙ NPDES discharge sites*

CANOE RATINGS

Surface Conditions

1. Smooth
2. Mostly smooth
3. Mixed smooth and rapid

4. Mostly rapid
x. not recommended
h. Passable only in high water

Aesthetics

a. Very attractive
b. Pleasant
c. Fair

*National Pollution Discharge Elimination System Permit Sites

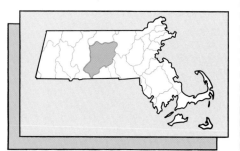

River Basin: Chicopee

Total Drainage Area: 721 sq. mi.
Drainage Area in MA: 721 sq. mi.
Source of River: Marshes at
  headwaters of Swift, Ware and
  Quaboag rivers
Mouth of River: Connecticut River
River Length in MA: 7.5 mi.
Major Tributaries: East Branch
  of the Swift River, Ware River
  and Quaboag River
Acres of Ponds, Lakes, Reservoirs:
  31,586 (Quabbin 25,000)
Hydropower Facilities:
  10; 17,840 kw
Wastewater Discharges:
  Municipal Treatment Plants 3
  Other 12
Features: Quabbin Reservoir,
  Belchertown Fish Hatchery,
  Quaboag Pond, Conant Brook
  Dam, Barre Falls Dam

Rare Species:

Plants: terete arrowhead, long-
  beaked bald-rush, golden club
Animals: common loon, American
  bald eagle #, four-toed
  salamander

\#   Federally Endangered

Chicopee River Basin

The Chicopee River is formed where its three tributaries—the Swift, the Ware and the Quaboag—meet at Palmer; its basin is the largest in the state.

The Swift River's three branches were impounded in 1938 to form the Quabbin Reservoir, the largest high quality water impoundment in the world. The 25,000 acre Quabbin Reservoir provides drinking water for Boston and 43 metropolitan area cities and towns. The Swift River below Quabbin remains an appealing cold water stream with good fishing. The state Division of Fisheries and Wildlife maintains the McLaughlin Fish Hatchery, one of the largest in the East, along the Swift River. It produces 200,000 trout annually for stream stocking.

The upper section of the Ware has Class A water which is seasonally diverted to the Quabbin Reservoir. Its midsection and lower reaches pursue a slow meandering course through evergreen and hardwood forests and support a healthy resident brown trout fishery.

The Quaboag, a much smaller river, begins in a broad marshy floodplain and ends in a pleasing series of rapids and pools. The river's midsection offers one of the best white water canoe trips in the state. Its upper and lower reaches provide good flat water canoeing.

The Chicopee eventually flows through the most populated area of the basin in Springfield where it empties into the larger Connecticut River. Six major hydropower facilities cause dramatic fluctuation in the water level, contributing to water quality problems.

Fifty-six thousand acres of publicly protected watershed land surrounding the Quabbin Reservoir, and twenty thousand acres of protected land in the Ware watershed provide excellent habitat for a variety of wildlife common to the state; few rare species are found in the basin since there are no particularly unusual geological or environmental features. Most of the reservoir is accessible for fishing. It yields more trophy-sized game species such as lake trout, brown trout and land-locked salmon than any other waterway in the state. The Chicopee hosts one of the most diversified fisheries in the state. Bass, northern pike, wild and stocked trout, as well as a wide variety of other species, can be found. The Division of Fisheries and Wildlife maintains an Atlantic salmon hatchery at Palmer to restore this much prized species to the Connecticut River. Northern pike and tiger muskie are also raised to augment the state's warm water fisheries.

A major American bald eagle restoration effort was established by the Division of Fisheries and Wildlife in 1982. As a result, two eagle pairs built nests at the Quabbin Reservoir in 1988, and the first eaglet hatching in Massachusetts since 1908 occurred in May of 1989.

American bald eagle at the Quabbin Reservoir

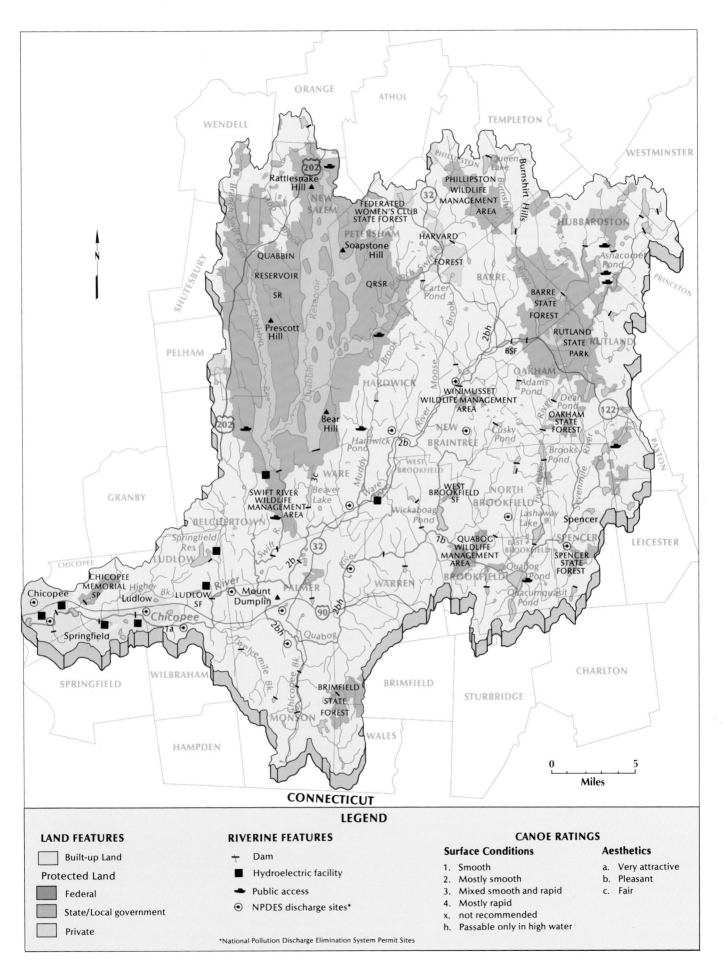

ORANGE ATHOL TEMPLETON WESTMINSTER

WENDELL

202
Rattlesnake
Hill ▲
NEW
SALEM
FEDERATED
WOMEN'S CLUB
STATE FOREST
PHILLIPSTON
WILDLIFE
MANAGEMENT
AREA
Burnshirt Hills
HUBBARDSTON

PHILLIPSTON
Queen
Lake
Burnshirt

32

PETERSHAM
HARVARD
FOREST
Soapstone
Hill ▲

QUABBIN
Carter
Pond
BARRE
Asnacomet
Pond
PRINCETON
RESERVOIR
SR
QRSR
E. Branch Swift River
Brook
BARRE
STATE
FOREST

2bh
RUTLAND
STATE
PARK
RUTLAND

Prescott
Hill ▲
Reservoir
BSF

202

Bear
Hill ▲

Brook
Moose
River
WINIMUSSET
WILDLIFE
MANAGEMENT
AREA
OAKHAM
Adams
Pond
Dean
Pond
OAKHAM
STATE
FOREST
122

HARDWICK

PELHAM

Quabbin Res.

Hardwick
Pond
2b
NEW
BRAINTREE
Cusky
Pond
Brooks
Pond

SHUTESBURY

GRANBY

Muddy
Brook
WEST
BROOKFIELD
WEST
BROOKFIELD
SF
NORTH
BROOKFIELD
Spencer
LEICESTER

SWIFT RIVER
WILDLIFE
MANAGEMENT
AREA
3c
WARE
Beaver
Lake
Ware River
Wickaboag
Pond
Lashaway
Lake
SPENCER
SPENCER
STATE
FOREST

BELCHERTOWN
Springfield
Res
7b
QUABOG
WILDLIFE
MANAGEMENT
AREA
EAST
BROOKFIELD

LUDLOW
Swift R.
32
River

CHICOPEE
MEMORIAL
SP
Higher
Bk.
LUDLOW
SF
Mount
Dumplin ▲
PALMER
Quabog
Pond
Quacumquasit
Pond
BROOKFIELD

Chicopee
River
WARREN

Springfield
Chicopee
1a
90
2bh
Quabog

2bh

Twelvemile Bk.

WILBRAHAM
Chicopee Bk.
BRIMFIELD
BRIMFIELD
STATE
FOREST
STURBRIDGE
CHARLTON

MONSON
WALES

HAMPDEN

0   5
Miles

CONNECTICUT

LEGEND

LAND FEATURES

- Built-up Land

Protected Land
- Federal
- State/Local government
- Private

RIVERINE FEATURES

- ┼ Dam
- ■ Hydroelectric facility
- ◄ Public access
- ⊙ NPDES discharge sites*

CANOE RATINGS

Surface Conditions
1. Smooth
2. Mostly smooth
3. Mixed smooth and rapid
4. Mostly rapid
x. not recommended
h. Passable only in high water

Aesthetics
a. Very attractive
b. Pleasant
c. Fair

*National Pollution Discharge Elimination System Permit Sites

47

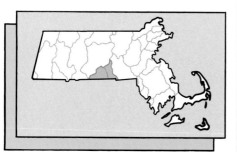

River Basin: Quinebaug and French

Total Drainage Area: 1,474 sq. mi.
Drainage Area in MA: 251 sq. mi.
Source of River:
  Quinebaug: brooks in western Brimfield and Wales
  French: ponds of Leicester and Spencer
Mouth of River:
  Quinebaug: Thames River
  French: Thames River
Total River Length:
  Quinebaug: 65 mi.
  French: 20.6 mi.
River Length in MA:
  Quinebaug: 18.7 mi.
  French: 14.4 mi.
Major Tributaries: Cady Brook, Little River, Mill Brook
Acres of Ponds, Lakes, Reservoirs: 5,999
Hydropower Facilities:
  Quinebaug: 2; 168 kw
  French: 1; 200 kw
Wastewater Discharges:
  Municipal Treatment Plants: Quinebaug 3; French 2
Features: Webster Lake, Brimfield State Forest, Old Sturbridge Village, Westville Lake, East Brimfield Lake, Hodges Village Dam, Buffumville Lake

Rare Species:

Plants: autumn coral root, purple clematis

Quinebaug & French River Basins

The Quinebaug River and the French River are both tributaries of the Thames River, which they join in the state of Connecticut. For their size, these river basins have many acres of lakes and ponds. The most notable lake is on the French River. It's one of the largest natural lakes in the state and has the longest name as well: Lake Chargoggagoggmanchaugagoggchaubunagungamuagg (to the native Americans it means "you fish on your side we fish on our side and nobody fishes in the middle.") Today it is known as Webster Lake. The basin's terrain has many hills cresting above 1,000 feet, but its geology is not particularly unusual. Therefore, the watershed does not harbor many rare species of plants or animals.

Both rivers were altered by federal flood control dams after major floods in 1955. Water quality problems exist due to previous and current industrial discharges and because of low flows and sedimentation in the impoundments. Major projects are now in progress to remedy these problems. The Quinebaug, which is stocked with brook, brown and rainbow trout, offers good sport fishing. The French offers pleasant, winding, slow waters, and particularly lovely scenery when fall color decorates the banks.

Both rivers were the sites of factories and mills during the early 1800's. Sturbridge Village, the historic reconstruction of the period, demonstrates several water powered mills which still use water from the Quinebaug today.

River in autumn

Whitetail deer

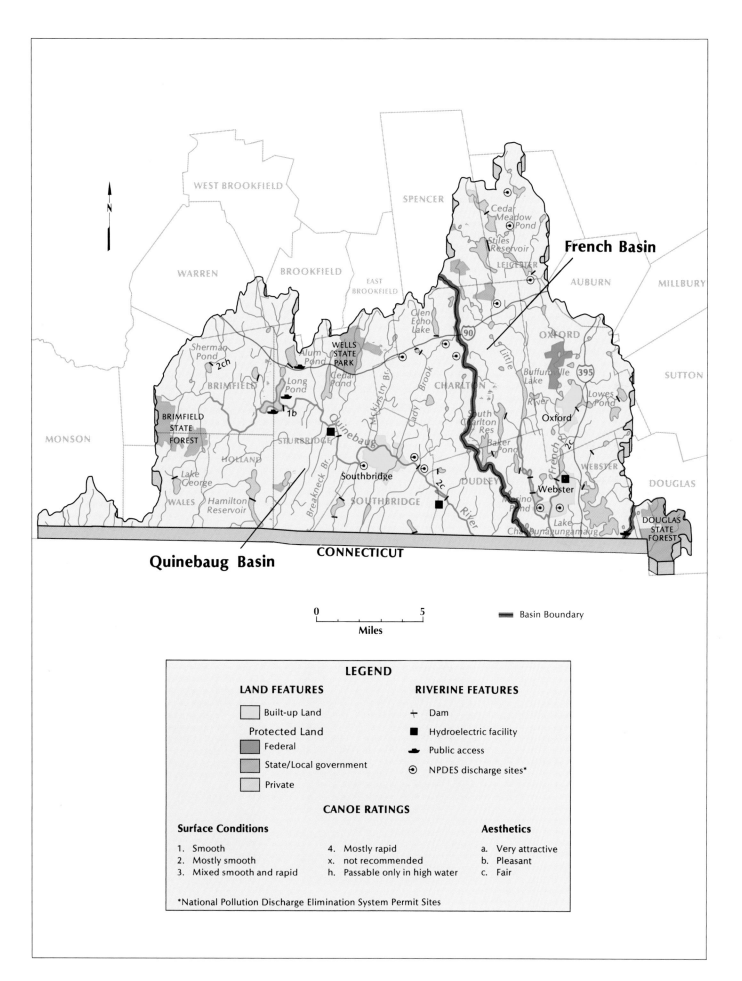

French Basin

Quinebaug Basin

CONNECTICUT

0　　　　　5

Miles

━━━ Basin Boundary

LEGEND

LAND FEATURES

▢ Built-up Land

Protected Land

▣ Federal

▣ State/Local government

▢ Private

RIVERINE FEATURES

╬ Dam

■ Hydroelectric facility

⬦ Public access

⊙ NPDES discharge sites*

CANOE RATINGS

Surface Conditions

1. Smooth
2. Mostly smooth
3. Mixed smooth and rapid

4. Mostly rapid
x. not recommended
h. Passable only in high water

Aesthetics

a. Very attractive
b. Pleasant
c. Fair

*National Pollution Discharge Elimination System Permit Sites

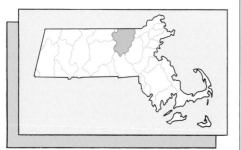

River Basin: Nashua

Total Drainage Area: 530 sq. mi.
Drainage Area in MA: 454 sq. mi.
Source of River: Wachusett
 Reservoir
Mouth of River: Merrimack River
Total River Length: 56 mi.
River Length in MA: 46 mi.
Major Tributaries: Squannacook
 River, Nissitissit River, Still-
 water River
Acres of Ponds, Lakes, Reservoirs:
6,818
Hydropower Facilities:
 2; 1,280 kw
Features: Wachusett Reservoir,
 Bolton Flats Wildlife Manage-
 ment Area, Mount Wachusett

Rare Species:

Plants: Bartram's shadbush,
 climbing fern, sand violet
Animals: pied-billed grebe,
 American bittern, Blanding's
 turtle

Nashua River Basin

The restoration of the Nashua River through citizen effort is one of the most impressive watershed protection stories the U.S. has ever seen. Twenty years ago, the Nashua was one of the ten most polluted rivers in the nation with less than 5% of its banks protected. Today, much of the Nashua has Class B water (fishable / swimmable). In addition, over 65% of its length and most of its major tributaries are protected as open space (see section V for details of the Nashua cleanup).

The Nashua's upper reaches have been impounded in Clinton to form the Wachusett Reservoir. Over 25 miles of surface and underground aqueduct connect the Quabbin Reservoir to the Wachusett Reservoir. An additional 30 miles of aqueduct transport water from the Wachusett Reservoir to Boston where it is used as an important part of the metropolitan water supply. Three major tributaries—the Stillwater, the Nissitissit and the Squannacook—are relatively wild and pristine. They offer excellent trout fishing, canoeing and opportunities to observe nature. The north branch and the entire main stem of the Nashua are popular canoe routes. The basin contains climates and soils which are quite typical of the state. However, its specialized habitats support a number of rare species.

The Nashua Basin contains four major state parks. One, Mount Wachusett, is a favorite local ski area in the winter. It is also a strategic location for viewing migrating red-tailed and broad-winged hawks. Numerous other public and private parks dot the basin.

Johnny Appleseed (John Chapman) was born on the banks of the North Nashua in Leominster. Benton MacKaye, founder of the Appalachian Trail, lived in Shirley and wrote much about the Squannacook River and why it should be protected.

The Nashua Basin has experienced significant growth in recent years, but it still retains many traditional farms and orchards. The restored Nashua has become an asset to this region's economy as well as to its environment.

Nashua River

A bellowing bullfrog

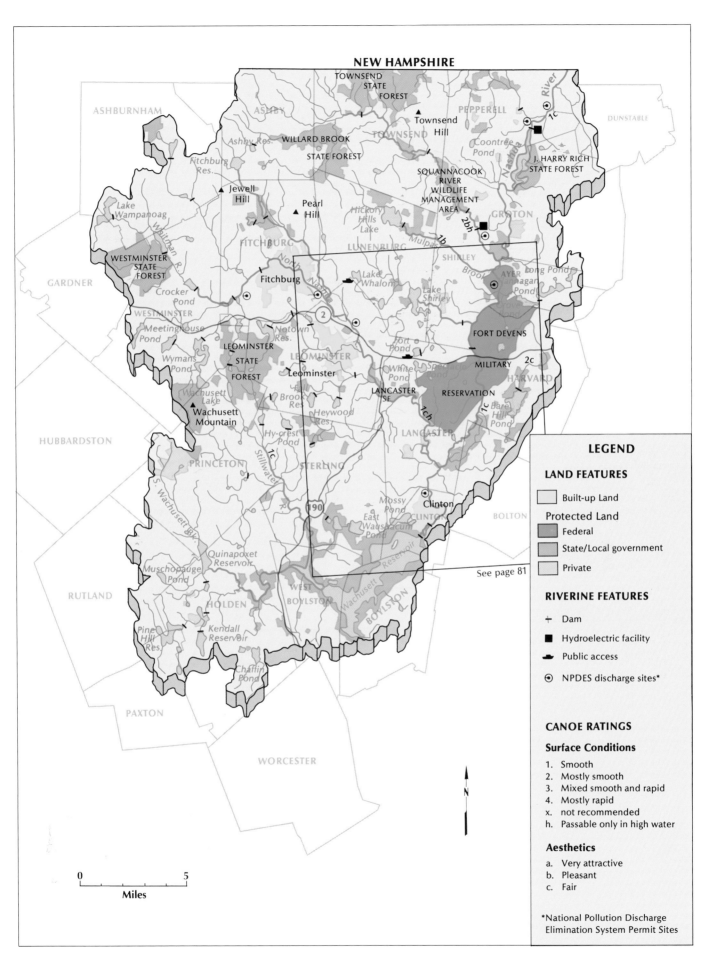

NEW HAMPSHIRE

TOWNSEND
STATE
FOREST

Townsend
Hill

ASHBY

WILLARD BROOK
STATE FOREST

TOWNSEND

PEPPERELL

Coontree
Pond

J. HARRY RICH
STATE FOREST

River

1c

ASHBURNHAM

DUNSTABLE

Ashby Res.

Fitchburg
Res.

Jewell
Hill

Pearl
Hill

Hickory
Hills
Lake

SQUANNACOOK
RIVER
WILDLIFE
MANAGEMENT
AREA

GROTON

2bh

1b

Mulpus

Nashua

Lake
Wampanoag

FITCHBURG

LUNENBURG

SHIRLEY

Brook

WESTMINSTER
STATE
FOREST

Crocker
Pond

Fitchburg

Lake
Whalom

Lake
Shirley

AYER

Long Pond

Sandy Pond

Grove Pond

North Nashua

GARDNER

WESTMINSTER

2

FORT DEVENS

2c

Meetinghouse
Pond

Notown
Res.

LEOMINSTER

Fort
Pond

Wymans
Pond

LEOMINSTER
STATE
FOREST

Leominster

White
Pond

MILITARY

HARVARD

Wachusett
Lake

Hall
Brook
Res.

LANCASTER
SE

RESERVATION

1ch

1c

Bare
Hill
Pond

Wachusett
Mountain

Heywood
Res.

LANCASTER

HUBBARDSTON

Hy-crest
Pond

1c

PRINCETON

Stillwater

STERLING

See page 81

S. Wachusett Bk.

190

Mossy
Pond

Clinton

BOLTON

East
Wausacum
Pond

CLINTON

Quinapoxet
Reservoir

Reservoir

Muschopauge
Pond

RUTLAND

HOLDEN

WEST
BOYLSTON

Wachusett

BOYLSTON

Pine
Hill
Res.

Kendall
Reservoir

Chaffin
Pond

PAXTON

WORCESTER

N

0   5
Miles

LEGEND

LAND FEATURES

◻ Built-up Land

Protected Land

◼ Federal

◼ State/Local government

◻ Private

RIVERINE FEATURES

✝ Dam

◼ Hydroelectric facility

➤ Public access

⊙ NPDES discharge sites*

CANOE RATINGS

Surface Conditions

1. Smooth
2. Mostly smooth
3. Mixed smooth and rapid
4. Mostly rapid
x. not recommended
h. Passable only in high water

Aesthetics

a. Very attractive
b. Pleasant
c. Fair

*National Pollution Discharge
Elimination System Permit Sites

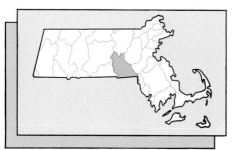

River Basin: Blackstone

Total Drainage Area: 640 sq. mi.
Drainage Area in MA: 382 sq. mi.
Source of River: streams in
  Worcester
Mouth of River: Narragansett
  Bay, Rhode Island
Total River Length: 40.3 mi.
River Length in MA: 27.9 mi.
Major Tributaries: Quinsigamond
  River, West River, Mumford
  River, Mill River
Acres of Ponds, Lakes, Reservoirs:
  7,097
Hydropower Facilities:
  1; 150 kw
Wastewater Discharges:
  Municipal Treatment Plants 6
  Other 3
Features: acid bogs, acidic wet-
  lands, Blackstone Gorge,
  Blackstone Heritage State Park,
  Purgatory Chasm State Park,
  King Philip's Rock, Douglas
  State Forest, West Hill Dam

Rare Species:

Plants: great laurel, grass-
  leaved ladies'-tresses, shining
  wedgegrass
Animals: marbled salamander,
  American brook lamprey, spotted turtle

Blackstone River Basin

The Blackstone River originates at a height of 1,300 feet along the slopes of Asnebumskit Hill in the Paxton / Holden area of Central Massachusetts. The river proceeds south into Rhode Island and eventually empties into Narragansett Bay, connecting the second and third largest population centers in New England: Worcester, Massachusetts and Providence, Rhode Island. The river has historically been one of the most heavily industrialized rivers in the country.

Named for Reverend William Blaxton (the first European resident of Boston and later the Blackstone Valley), the river was soon developed for industry because of the series of steep drops along its route which provided excellent conditions for water power. The Blackstone Valley has been called "the birthplace of America's Industrial Revolution" because, in 1790, the nation's first textile mill was established in Pawtucket, Rhode Island. Upstream, the Blackstone Canal was constructed in the 1820's to carry passengers and freight between Worcester and Providence. Competition from the railroads made the canal's use short-lived, but industrialization continued. At one time, all but thirty feet (out of 430 feet) of vertical falls along the river from Worcester to Pawtucket were harnessed for mill power, and thus, the river gained the reputation of being "America's hardest working river."

With the demise of the textile industry, all that survived of the mill era was a severely polluted river that remained ignored and abused for decades. Major strides in cleanup have been made since the late 1970's, but serious problems still remain. Sediments left by industry, nonpoint source pollution from urban runoff and inadequate wastewater treatment present continuing challenges to the Blackstone River Watershed Association and other advocates for river corridor protection. However, the formation of the new Blackstone River Valley National Heritage Corridor (a joint venture between Massachusetts, Rhode Island and the National Park Service) and the vigilance of other local groups leave hope of a promising future for the river.

Rice City Pond, site of the Heritage
Homecoming Canoe Race

Blackstone River

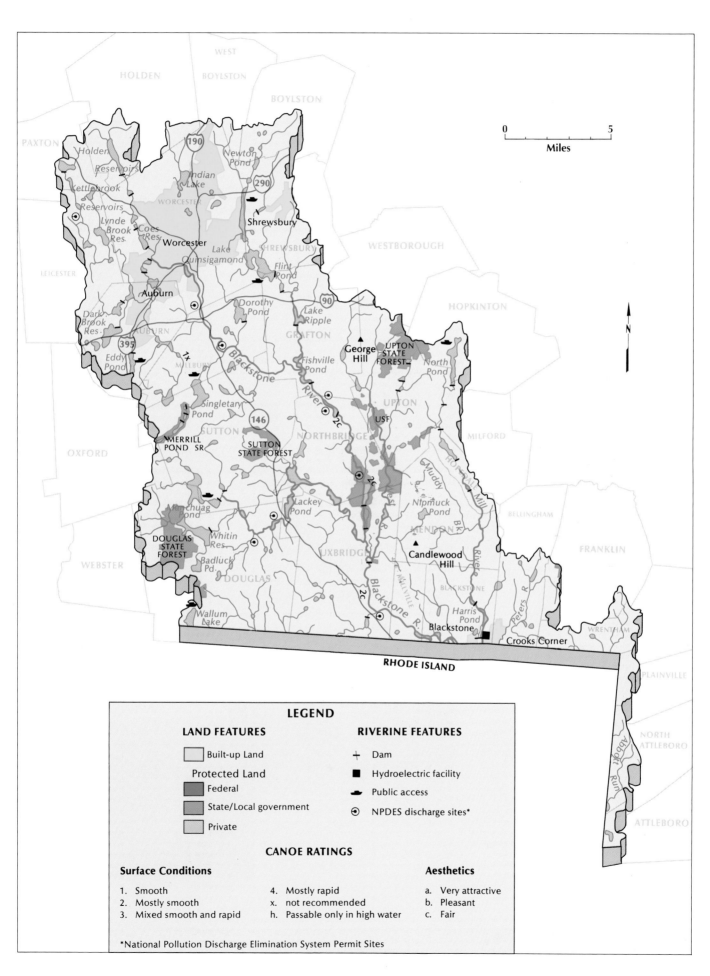

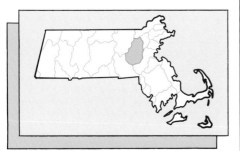

River Basin: Concord, Assabet, Sudbury

Total Drainage Area: 377 sq. mi.
Drainage Area in MA: 377 sq. mi.
Source of River:
 Concord: Assabet and Sudbury rivers
 Assabet: Little Bummet Brook
 Sudbury: Cedar Swamp
Mouth of River:
 Concord: Merrimack River
 Assabet: Concord River
 Sudbury: Concord River
River Length in MA:
 Concord: 15.5 mi.
 Assabet: 29.8 mi.
 Sudbury: 28.8 mi.
Major Tributaries: Fort Pond Brook, Assabet Brook, Wash Brook
Acres of Ponds, Lakes, Reservoirs: 7,478
Hydropower Facilities:
 Concord 1; 675 kw
 Assabet 3; 303 kw
Features: Great Meadows National Wildlife Refuge, Walden Pond State Reservation, Old Grist Mill in Sudbury, Minuteman National Historic Park (Old North Bridge), Egg Rock

Rare Species:

Plants: river bulrush, Britton's violet, violet wood-sorrel
Animals: blue-spotted salamander, American bittern, common moorhen

Concord, Assabet & Sudbury River Basins

The Concord-Assabet-Sudbury Basin is a major tributary network of the Merrimack River. Before joining the Merrimack at Lowell, these rivers traverse a variety of terrain and change character several times. The Sudbury is the longest branch in the system. At its upper end, it is a narrow, rapidly flowing stream checked by a few small impoundments. In Framingham, the river has been impounded by two large dams. In its lower section, it takes on an entirely different character—slow, meadow-lined, with a drop in elevation of a mere foot for twelve miles. This stretch is protected in the Great Meadows National Wildlife Refuge which has abundant waterfowl and excellent bass fishing.

The Assabet is a smaller river; rockier and narrower with a steeper gradient. At its headwaters, wetlands were impounded for flood control, creating a rookery for great blue heron. The river's faster flow made its shore a desirable location for water-powered grist mills. By the 1960's, suburban sprawl had made the Assabet one of the most degraded rivers in the state. However, new sewage treatment plants are improving water quality.

In Concord, where the Sudbury and Assabet meet, the Concord River begins. This slow-moving river winds its way through wide meadows and pleasant suburban and rural countryside until it reaches the city of Lowell. At this point, it enters the Merrimack. Water quality conditions are improving in sections of the Concord which do not yet meet federal standards.

Native Americans planted crops on the banks of the Concord and fished its waters. Its valley is full of reminders of early colonial history. The North Bridge, which crosses the river in the town of Concord, was the site of the "shot heard 'round the world." Later, the Concord River was immortalized in the writings of Thoreau and Emerson. Walden Pond, Thoreau's wilderness retreat, is now a popular state park.

Canoeing on the Sudbury River

Great blue herons

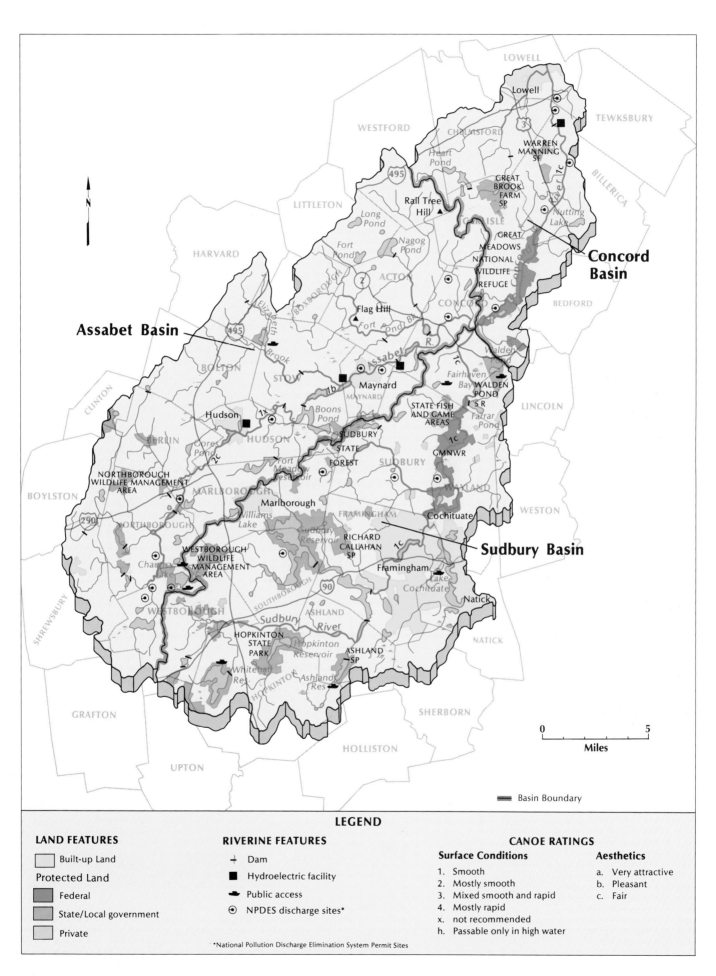

Concord Basin

Assabet Basin

Sudbury Basin

LOWELL

WESTFORD

CHELMSFORD

TEWKSBURY

BILLERICA

WARREN MANNING SF

Heart Pond

GREAT BROOK FARM SP

Rail Tree Hill

Long Pond

Nagog Pond

Fort Pond

Nutting Lake

CARLISLE

GREAT MEADOWS NATIONAL WILDLIFE REFUGE

Concord River 1c

HARVARD

LITTLETON

ACTON

BOXBOROUGH

Flag Hill

Fort Pond Br.

CONCORD

BEDFORD

Elizabeth Brook

Assabet R.

Walden Pond

Fairhaven Bay

WALDEN POND SR

BOLTON

STOW

1b

Maynard

MAYNARD

STATE FISH AND GAME AREAS

Farrar Pond

LINCOLN

Hudson

1x

Boons Pond

1c

CLINTON

BERLIN

HUDSON

Gates Pond

SUDBURY STATE FOREST

SUDBURY

GMNWR

WAYLAND

2c

Fort Meadow Reservoir

NORTHBOROUGH WILDLIFE MANAGEMENT AREA

MARLBOROUGH

BOYLSTON

Williams Lake

Marlborough

FRAMINGHAM

Cochituate

WESTON

290

NORTHBOROUGH

Sudbury Reservoir

RICHARD CALLAHAN SP

1c

WESTBOROUGH WILDLIFE MANAGEMENT AREA

Chauncy Lake

Framingham

Lake Cochituate

Natick

SHREWSBURY

WESTBOROUGH

SOUTHBOROUGH

90

ASHLAND

NATICK

Sudbury River

HOPKINTON STATE PARK

Hopkinton Reservoir

ASHLAND SP

Whitehall Res.

HOPKINTON

Ashland Res.

SHERBORN

GRAFTON

HOLLISTON

UPTON

N

0   5
Miles

Basin Boundary

LEGEND

LAND FEATURES

Built-up Land

Protected Land

Federal

State/Local government

Private

RIVERINE FEATURES

+ Dam

■ Hydroelectric facility

Public access

⊙ NPDES discharge sites*

*National Pollution Discharge Elimination System Permit Sites

CANOE RATINGS

Surface Conditions

1. Smooth
2. Mostly smooth
3. Mixed smooth and rapid
4. Mostly rapid
x. not recommended
h. Passable only in high water

Aesthetics

a. Very attractive
b. Pleasant
c. Fair

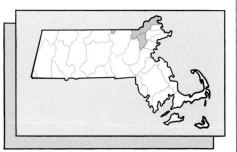

River Basin: Merrimack and Shawsheen

Total Drainage Area:
  Merrimack: 5,010 sq. mi.
  Shawsheen: 77 sq. mi.
Drainage Area in MA:
  Merrimack: 1,210 sq. mi.
  Shawsheen: 77 sq. mi.
Source of River:
  Merrimack: Near Franklin, NH
  Shawsheen: Bedford
Mouth of River:
  Merrimack: Atlantic Ocean
  at Newburyport
  Shawsheen: Merrimack River
Total River Length:
  Merrimack: 134 mi.
  Shawsheen: 25 mi.
River Length in MA:
  Merrimack: 45.2 mi.
  Shawsheen: 25 mi.
Major Tributaries: Nashua River,
  Concord River, Spicket River
Acres of Ponds, Lakes, Reservoirs:
  18,875
Hydropower Facilities:
  Merrimack River: 10; 41,303 kw
  Spicket River: 1; 357 kw
Wastewater Discharges:
  Municipal Treatment Plants 6
  Other 6
Features: Carr Island Wildlife
  Sanctuary, Ram Island Wildlife
  Sanctuary, Lowell Heritage State
  Park, annual shad run

Merrimack & Shawsheen River Basins

About three-quarters of the Merrimack River is located in New Hampshire. It enters Massachusetts in Tyngsboro. In Lowell it turns and flows to the Atlantic at Newburyport. The last nine miles of the river is an estuary that drains 4,028 acres of salt marsh. This is one of the largest marshes in the state and an invaluable "nursery" for freshwater and marine fish as well as other animal species. The estuary includes the best freshwater tidal wetlands in the state.

The Merrimack contains some unusual plant specimens. For example, its floodplains are the primary natural location of river birch in the state. An island in the Merrimack has silverling (a woody stemmed wildflower), the only occurrence of this species outside of northern New Hampshire. It is believed that the ancestors of these plants were washed down river from the New Hampshire mountains.

The Merrimack has long suffered from municipal and industrial pollution and most of the river still does not meet its federal classification. As a result, the once enormously productive shellfish industry, in the tidal flats near the river's mouth, has been shut down.

The river offers a good deal of enjoyable canoeing through varied countryside. Particularly in the marshlands, canoeists can enjoy a multitude of bird and other wildlife sightings. The Division of Fisheries and Wildlife, the Division of Marine Fisheries and the U.S. Fish and Wildlife Service are working on a major restoration effort for Atlantic salmon, American shad and other anadromous fish. The Lowell Heritage State Park (the first urban national park of its kind) preserves examples of a textile mill era that had a dramatic impact on the region and the world's economy. The success of the park relies heavily on the beauty of the Merrimack and an elaborate canal system that passes through Lowell.

The Shawsheen River is a major tributary of the Merrimack. Most of the river meets Class B standards (fishable / swimmable) for water quality, although pollution problems due primarily to small wastewater discharges and urban runoff persist in towns such as Andover and South Lawrence. Despite these problems and growing development pressures, the slow-moving river flows through many wildlife-rich freshwater marshes.

Rare Species:

Plants: silverling ●, seabeach dock, seabeach needlegrass, estuary pipewort
Animals: common tern, golden-winged warbler, American bald eagle #

●   Endangered in Massachusetts
Federally Endangered

Fishing on the Merrimack River

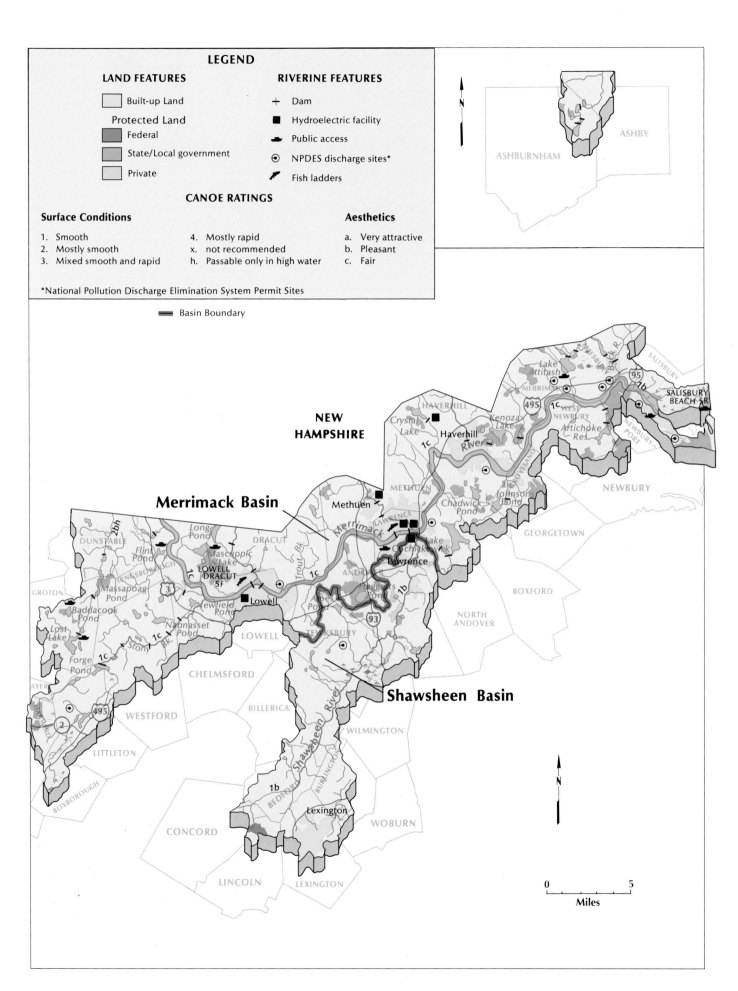

LEGEND

LAND FEATURES

- Built-up Land

Protected Land
- Federal
- State/Local government
- Private

RIVERINE FEATURES

- ╋ Dam
- ■ Hydroelectric facility
- Public access
- ⊙ NPDES discharge sites*
- Fish ladders

CANOE RATINGS

Surface Conditions

1. Smooth
2. Mostly smooth
3. Mixed smooth and rapid
4. Mostly rapid
x. not recommended
h. Passable only in high water

Aesthetics

a. Very attractive
b. Pleasant
c. Fair

*National Pollution Discharge Elimination System Permit Sites

━━ Basin Boundary

ASHBURNHAM

ASHBY

NEW HAMPSHIRE

HAVERHILL

Crystal Lake

Lake Attitash

Kenoza Lake

Merrimack River

Artichoke Res.

SALISBURY BEACH SF

Haverhill

WEST NEWBURY

NEWBURYPORT

NEWBURY

Merrimack Basin

Methuen

METHUEN

Chadwick Pond

Johnsons Pond

GEORGETOWN

Lawrence

LAWRENCE

Lake Cochickewick

ANDOVER

BOXFORD

DUNSTABLE

DRACUT

Long Pond

Trout Bk.

Flint Pond

Mascuppic Lake

LOWELL DRACUT SF

Newfield Pond

Ayers Pond

Fregeolles Pond

NORTH ANDOVER

GROTON

TYNGSBOROUGH

Massapoag Pond

Baddacook Pond

Lowell

LOWELL

Nabnasset Pond

Stony Bk.

TEWKSBURY

Shawsheen Basin

Lost Lake

Forge Pond

CHELMSFORD

WILMINGTON

WESTFORD

BILLERICA

Shawsheen River

AYER

LITTLETON

BOXBOROUGH

BEDFORD

BURLINGTON

WOBURN

CONCORD

Lexington

LINCOLN

LEXINGTON

0   5
Miles

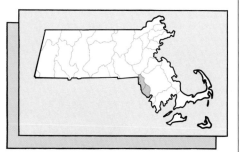

River Basin:
Ten Mile and
Narragansett Bay

Total Drainage Area: 104.6 sq. mi.
Drainage Area in MA: 104.6 sq. mi.
Source of River:
  Ten Mile: Cargill Pond
Mouth of River:
  Ten Mile: Narragansett Bay
River Length in MA:
  Ten Mile: 15 mi.
Major Tributaries: Sevenmile
  River, Fourmile Brook, Bungay
  River
Acres of Ponds, Lakes, Reservoirs:
  Ten Mile: 1,301
  Narragansett Bay: 146

Features: North Attleborough Fish
  Hatchery, Warren Upper Reservoir, Watson Pond State Park

Rare Species:

Plants: Plymouth gentian, climbing
  fern, two-flowered bladderwort,
  Eaton's beggar-ticks

Ten Mile & Narragansett Bay Basins

The Ten Mile River Basin has been a center of industrial development for over 200 years, particularly in the jewelry manufacturing field. Through the years heavy metals and toxins were left in the entire river. This caused serious water quality problems in the Ten Mile River and the Seekonk River, which flows into Narragansett Bay. Recent development in both the Ten Mile and Narragansett watersheds has mirrored the heavy growth patterns in eastern Massachusetts, adding even more pressures on the natural resources in these basins.

However, significant progress has been made in reducing pollution problems in recent years. Sewage treatment and industrial waste treatment improved dramatically in the 1960's and early 1970's under a program governed by the U.S. Environmental Protection Agency (EPA) and the Massachusetts Department of Environmental Quality Engineering (DEQE). Discharge limitations for toxic metals, established by the EPA and DEQE in 1984, have dramatically reduced toxic discharges as well.

Today, the major problem which still needs to be addressed is the preponderance of heavily contaminated sediment in the river beds. The cleanup will be environmentally difficult and expensive, but necessary if the Ten Mile and other rivers are to become viable assets for the region.

Ten Mile River in North Attleboro

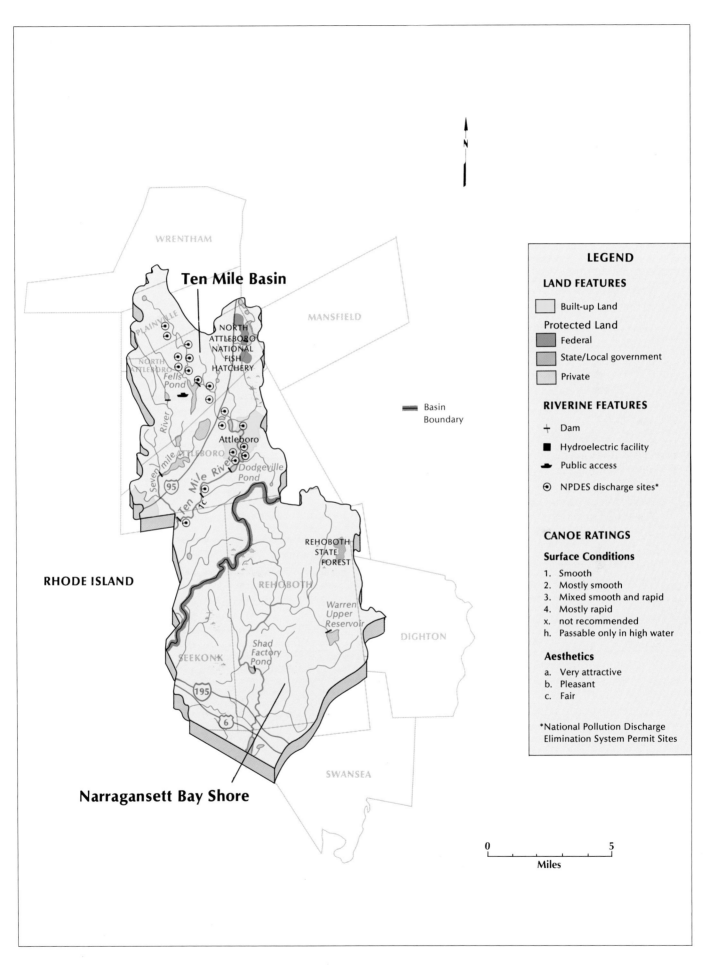

Ten Mile Basin

WRENTHAM

MANSFIELD

PLAINVILLE

NORTH
ATTLEBORO
NATIONAL
FISH
HATCHERY

NORTH
ATTLEBORO

Fells
Pond

Seven mile River

ATTLEBORO

Attleboro

95

Ten Mile River

Dodgeville
Pond

RHODE ISLAND

REHOBOTH
STATE
FOREST

REHOBOTH

Warren
Upper
Reservoir

DIGHTON

SEEKONK

Shad
Factory
Pond

195

6

SWANSEA

Narragansett Bay Shore

LEGEND

LAND FEATURES

Built-up Land

Protected Land

Federal

State/Local government

Private

RIVERINE FEATURES

$+$ Dam

■ Hydroelectric facility

 Public access

⊙ NPDES discharge sites*

 Basin
Boundary

CANOE RATINGS

Surface Conditions

1. Smooth
2. Mostly smooth
3. Mixed smooth and rapid
4. Mostly rapid
x. not recommended
h. Passable only in high water

Aesthetics

a. Very attractive
b. Pleasant
c. Fair

*National Pollution Discharge
Elimination System Permit Sites

0   5

Miles

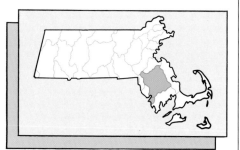

River Basin:
Taunton and
Mount Hope Bay

Total Drainage Area: 1,052.8 sq. mi.
Drainage Area in MA: 713.8 sq. mi.
Source of River:
  Taunton: ponds and brooks in,
  Easton, Avon, Stoughton,
  Holbrook
Mouth of River:
  Taunton: Mount Hope Bay
River Length in MA:
  Taunton: 48.9 mi.
Major Tributaries: Matfield River,
Assonet River, Fourmile Brook,
Town River
Acres of Ponds, Lakes, Reservoirs:
17,763
Features: Hockomock Swamp
Wildlife Management Area,
Dighton Rock State Park,
Wamponoag canoe passage

Rare Species:

Plants: Plymouth gentian,
climbing fern, two-flowered bladderwort, Eaton's beggar's-tick
Animals: blue-spotted salamander,
upland sandpiper ●, northern
parula, eastern box turtle

● Endangered in Massachusetts

Taunton & Mount Hope Bay River Basins

The Taunton River Basin is the second largest drainage area in Massachusetts. The river has one of the flattest courses in the state with only a twenty foot difference along the forty mile length of the main stem. Its level terrain creates extensive wetlands throughout the basin, including the 6,000 acre Hockomock Swamp, one of the largest wetlands in New England.

Saltwater intrusion occurs as far as twelve miles upstream with tidal changes notice-able eighteen miles upstream. These conditions influence vegetation and wildlife along the river. The Taunton remains fairly uniform in width within its freshwater portion, then broadens into an estuary. Its watershed is notable for the myriad of small tributaries throughout the basin. Still, the overall condition of the basin is some-what dry. However, the watershed's limited wetlands support a large diversity of rare plants and animals.

The river has suffered considerably from pollution. New treatment plants and other improvements have made measurable differences in water quality and have created new opportunities for enjoyment of the river. While the river's warm waters do not support trout or other prized fish, the Taunton does have anadromous fish such as alewives and shad which provide exciting recreational fishing opportunities. A newly formed citizens group is working on repairing key fish ladders to restore the ana-dromous fish runs and to revive interest in the river as a vital resource for the region.

The Taunton River flows into Mount Hope Bay, a watershed which experiences water quality problems typical of an urban drainage system. Even though the city of Fall River's primary wastewater treatment plant was upgraded in 1983, both the Lee and Cole rivers experience high fecal coliform bacteria counts, especially after major rainstorms. The pollution problems limit recreational opportunities and have caused many shellfish bed closures in the estuaries of tidally-influenced rivers throughout the basin.

Hockomock River in Taunton

Eastern box turtle

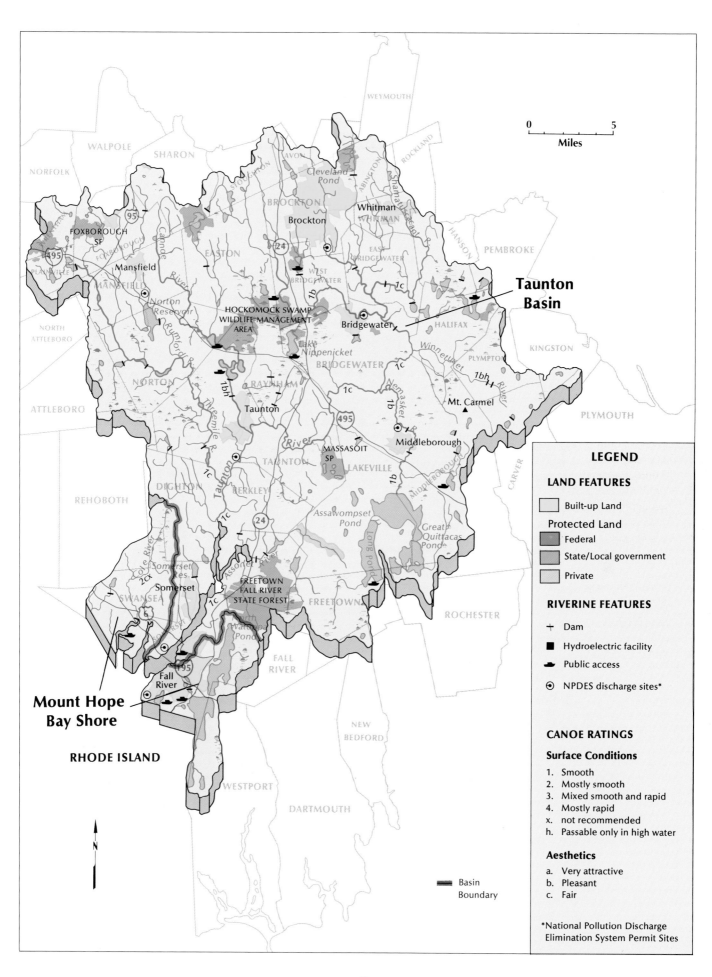

Taunton Basin

Mount Hope Bay Shore

RHODE ISLAND

LEGEND

LAND FEATURES

Built-up Land

Protected Land

Federal

State/Local government

Private

RIVERINE FEATURES

+ Dam

■ Hydroelectric facility

Public access

⊙ NPDES discharge sites*

CANOE RATINGS

Surface Conditions

1. Smooth
2. Mostly smooth
3. Mixed smooth and rapid
4. Mostly rapid
x. not recommended
h. Passable only in high water

Aesthetics

a. Very attractive
b. Pleasant
c. Fair

*National Pollution Discharge Elimination System Permit Sites

Basin Boundary

0   Miles   5

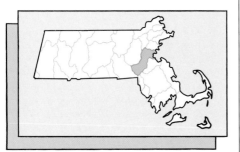

River Basin: Charles

Total Drainage Area: 307 sq. mi.
Drainage Area in MA: 307 sq. mi.
Source of River: A spring on
  Honey Hill in Hopkinton
Mouth of River: Boston Harbor
River Length in MA: 80 mi.
Major Tributaries: Hopping
  Brook, Mill River, Stony Brook
Acres of Ponds, Lakes, Reservoirs:
  4,388
Features: 20,000 acres of wet-
  lands, Charles Bank Park,
  Emerald Necklace Park System,
  9-mile long Charles Basin,
  pumping station at Prison Point
  in Charlestown

Rare Species:

Plants: great laurel, arethusa,
  river bulrush
Animals: blue-spotted salamander,
  spotted turtle

Charles River Basin

The Charles River is the longest river in the state. It begins at a spring on Honey Hill in Hopkinton and follows an 80-mile meandering course (its Indian name was "Quinobequin" for "meandering river") through relatively rural areas, at first, and then through the metropolitan Boston area.

Despite much development, the basin still contains over 20,000 acres of wetlands. Much of the stream corridor is protected and supports a variety of native wetland plant species, birds and other wildlife. The extensive wetlands also provide "natural valley storage" for floodwaters.

Based on citizen input, the U.S. Army Corps of Engineers purchased much of the open space for the purpose of nonstructural flood control. These open spaces (particularly the Charles River Meadows in Dedham and Needham) are very important to wildlife and provide a model for alternative flood control in other basins.

Once a public nuisance because of poor water quality, the Charles has more recently been nicknamed "the People's River" because of intensive citizen efforts mounted over the last fifteen years on its behalf. Events such as the Head of the Charles rowing competition and the annual Charles River canoe race attract participants from around the world.

Clearly, the river has become the major recreational waterway in the metropolitan Boston area. Its upper portions are particularly fine for canoeing year-round, and the protected portions of its floodplain offer nature lovers and outdoor enthusiasts relief from the otherwise densely urban character of the Charles.

Sailing on the Charles River

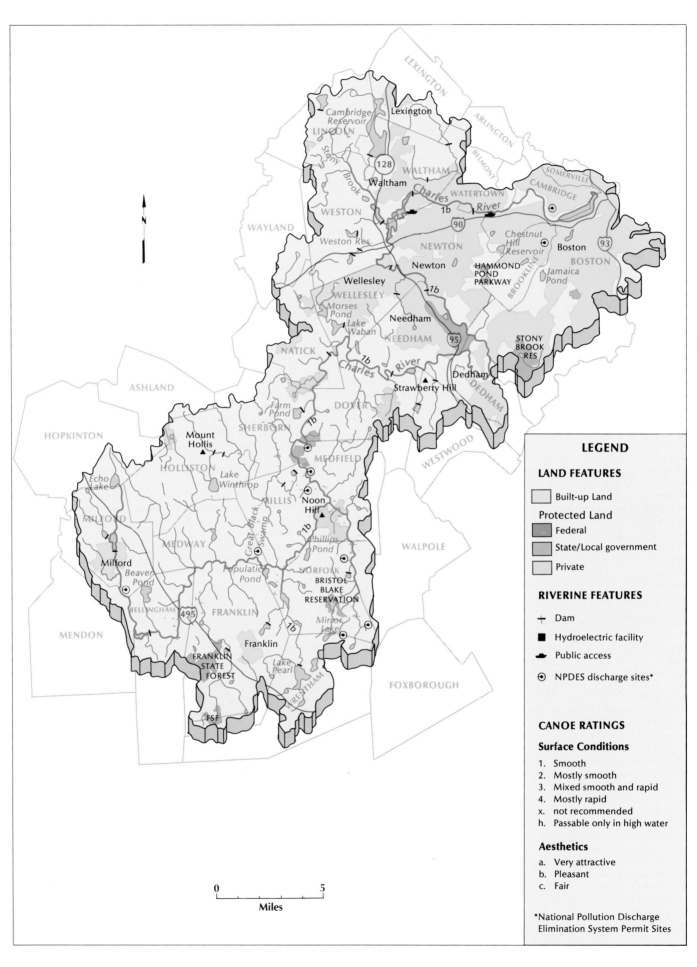

LEGEND

LAND FEATURES

▢ Built-up Land

Protected Land

▢ Federal

▢ State/Local government

▢ Private

RIVERINE FEATURES

+ Dam

■ Hydroelectric facility

⬗ Public access

⊙ NPDES discharge sites*

CANOE RATINGS

Surface Conditions

1. Smooth
2. Mostly smooth
3. Mixed smooth and rapid
4. Mostly rapid
x. not recommended
h. Passable only in high water

Aesthetics

a. Very attractive
b. Pleasant
c. Fair

*National Pollution Discharge Elimination System Permit Sites

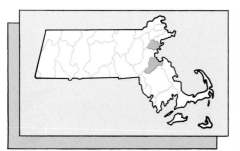

River Basin:
Boston Harbor

Total Drainage Area: 261 sq. mi.
Drainage Area in MA: 261 sq. mi.
River Lengths in MA:
  Mystic River: 17 mi.
  Neponset River: 30 mi.
  Weymouth River: 12 mi.
  Weir River: 12 mi.
Major Tributaries: Aberjona
  River, Monatiquot River
Acres of Ponds, Lakes, Reservoirs:
  7,601
Features: Boston Harbor Islands
  State Park, Middlesex Fells,
  Land's End Reservation, Fowl
  Meadow

Rare Species:

Plants: knotted pearlwort, pale
  green orchis, lesser snakeroot ●
Animals: least tern, common tern,
  spotted turtle, Mystic Valley
  amphipod, least bittern, northern
  copperhead ●

●   Endangered in Massachusetts

Boston Harbor Basin

In addition to the Charles River, three other major rivers empty into Boston Harbor. The Neponset River, which begins in Foxboro as an artificial reservoir, is impounded by a number of dams built by industries over the years. On the Quincy / Milton line, just below the last dam, the river flows into and nourishes a large estuarine marsh, some of which is still intact despite the recent development of the basin. Fowl Meadow is another significant feature of the basin. It spans 8 towns and 3,000 acres, but only 500 acres are protected in public ownership. The important aquifer, over which the Meadow lies, is still threatened by encroachment. These marshes and meadows are important stopover areas for migratory birds. The 5,000 acre Blue Hills Reservation is also located in this basin. Rare plants and animal species can still be found here. Pokapog Bog, just to the south of the hills, hosts an Atlantic white cedar swamp.

The Neponset River suffers terribly from diverse sources of pollution. Industry, development and acid rain all adversely impact the basin's diminishing wetlands. However, remaining wetlands support a wide variety of plants and animals, and newly protected open spaces along the river are being developed for a recreational park system by the Metropolitan District Commission.

The Weymouth and Weir rivers are among the many small creeks and streams that make up the Boston Harbor Basin. Both of these rivers are influenced by tides and flow into Hingham Harbor. Unfortunately, the largely urban character of the area causes many water quality problems.

The Mystic River is another even more urbanized stream that enters Boston Harbor from the north. The river is heavily controlled by dams built for flow control and to halt saltwater intrusion. As with the other rivers in this basin, water quality is poor. The Mystic River and Mystic Lakes region is a pleasant recreational resource for the area, but much work is required before its full potential can be realized.

Fowl Meadow

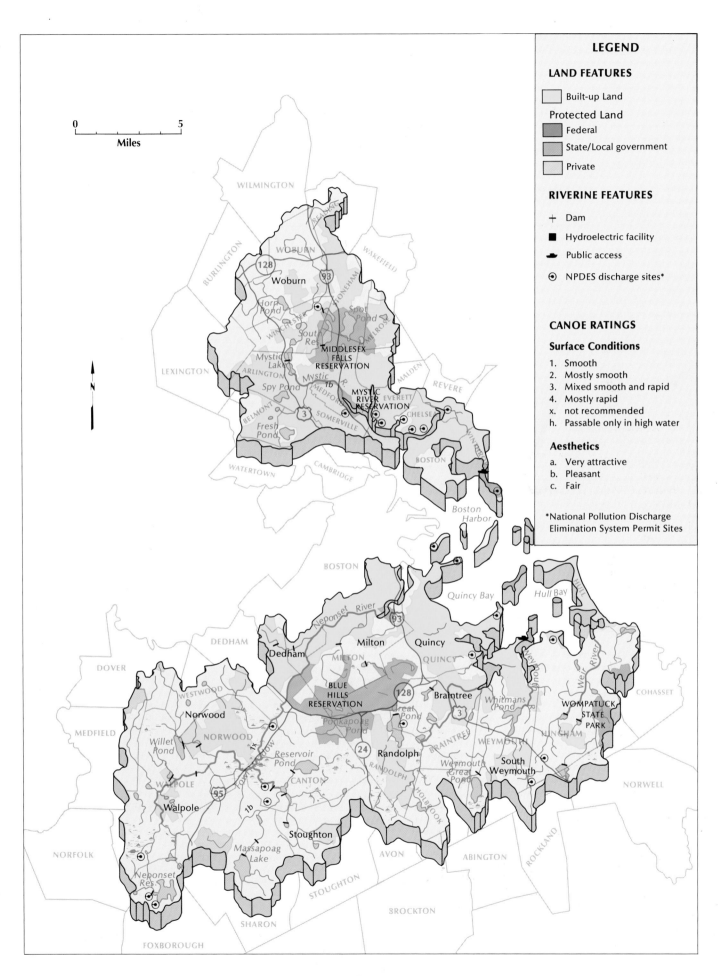

LEGEND

LAND FEATURES

Built-up Land

Protected Land

Federal

State/Local government

Private

RIVERINE FEATURES

+ Dam

■ Hydroelectric facility

Public access

⊙ NPDES discharge sites*

CANOE RATINGS

Surface Conditions

1. Smooth
2. Mostly smooth
3. Mixed smooth and rapid
4. Mostly rapid
x. not recommended
h. Passable only in high water

Aesthetics

a. Very attractive
b. Pleasant
c. Fair

*National Pollution Discharge Elimination System Permit Sites

0 —— 5
Miles

N

WILMINGTON

BURLINGTON

WOBURN

WAKEFIELD

128

93

Woburn

Horn Pond

STONEHAM

Spot Pond

MELROSE

WINCHESTER

South Res.

LEXINGTON

Mystic Lake

ARLINGTON

MEDFORD

MIDDLESEX FELLS RESERVATION

Mystic R.

MALDEN

REVERE

Spy Pond

1b

MYSTIC RIVER RESERVATION

EVERETT

3

SOMERVILLE

CHELSEA

BELMONT

Fresh Pond

WINTHROP

WATERTOWN

CAMBRIDGE

BOSTON

Boston Harbor

BOSTON

Neponset River

Quincy Bay

Hull Bay

93

HULL

DEDHAM

Milton

Quincy

Dedham

MILTON

QUINCY

DOVER

WESTWOOD

Weir River

COHASSET

Norwood

BLUE HILLS RESERVATION

128

Braintree

Whitmans Pond

WOMPATUCK STATE PARK

NORWOOD

Ponkapoag Pond

3

Great Pond

BRAINTREE

WEYMOUTH

HINGHAM

MEDFIELD

Willet Pond

Reservoir Pond

24

Randolph

Weymouth Great Pond

South Weymouth

WALPOLE

95

CANTON

RANDOLPH

HOLBROOK

NORWELL

Walpole

1b

Stoughton

AVON

ABINGTON

ROCKLAND

NORFOLK

Massapoag Lake

Neponset Res.

STOUGHTON

BROCKTON

SHARON

FOXBOROUGH

65

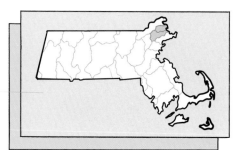

River Basin:
Parker and Ipswich

Total Drainage Area: 245 sq. mi.
Drainage Area in MA: 245 sq. mi.
Source of River:
  Parker: brooks in Boxford and
  Baldpate Pond
  Ipswich: wetlands and Mill Pond
  in Burlington
River Length in MA:
  Parker: 19.1 mi.
  Ipswich: 30.5 mi.
Major Tributaries: Penn Brook,
  Mill River, Fish Brook, Lubbers
  Brook
Acres of Ponds, Lakes, Reservoirs:
  2,298
Major Dams: Ipswich River 3
Wastewater Discharges:
  Ipswich River:
    Municipal Treatment Plants 1
    Other 9
Features: Plum Island State Park,
  Parker River National Wildlife
  Refuge, Willowdale State Forest,
  extensive salt marshes

Rare Species:

Plants: estuary arrowhead ●,
  seabeach needlegrass
Animals: blue-spotted salamander,
  golden-winged warbler, piping
  plover +, Blanding's turtle

●   Endangered in Massachusetts
+   Federally Threatened

Parker & Ipswich River Basins

The Parker River and the Ipswich River are adjacent river basins in the northeast corner of the state which drain into the Atlantic. The Ipswich River winds through wetlands dotted by glacial drumlins or small hillocks. A dozen towns rely on this river for water. Since groundwater supplies the base flow for the system, withdrawals from municipal and private wells greatly affect water levels in the river. However, its importance as a water supply has led to protections that guard against contamination.

The Parker is a small, still, pristine river that meanders through meadows until—after a series of dams—it becomes brackish. The river flows into Plum Island Sound, where some 4,650 acres of beautiful coastal salt marsh, sand dunes and freshwater marsh have been protected in the Parker River National Wildlife Refuge. Plum Island, with its wildlife, myriad of bird species, wild roses, beach plums, and white sand beaches, has become one of the North Shore's greatest attractions. This area is the site of the largest salt marsh in the state. The marsh, dunes and barrier beach spread over some 23,790 acres which have been designated as an "Area of Critical Environmental Concern" by the state. Efforts are now being made to limit increasing human intrusion into important shore bird nesting areas.

The estuarine habitat provided by both rivers is important to marine species, rare land animals and plants. More rare species are expected to be found when thorough inventories are completed.

Egrets and herons feeding at Parker River

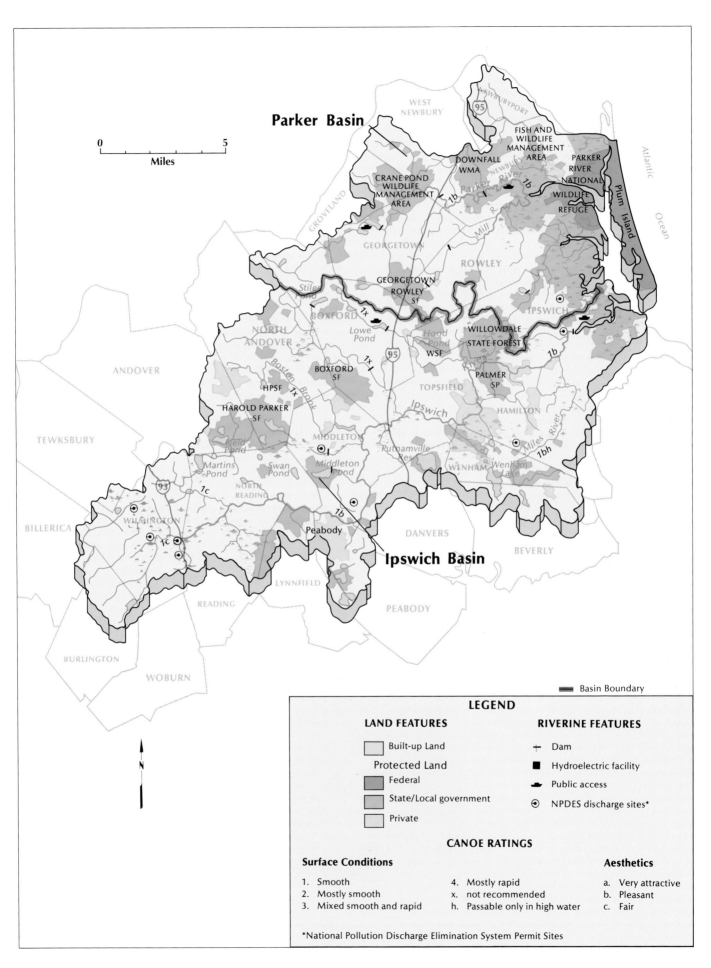

Parker Basin

Ipswich Basin

WEST NEWBURY

FISH AND WILDLIFE MANAGEMENT AREA

DOWNFALL WMA

PARKER RIVER NATIONAL WILDLIFE REFUGE

CRANE POND WILDLIFE MANAGEMENT AREA

Atlantic

Ocean

Plum Island

GROVELAND

Parker River

Newbury River

Mill River

GEORGETOWN

ROWLEY

1b

1b

GEORGETOWN ROWLEY SF

Stiles Pond

BOXFORD

1x

IPSWICH

NORTH ANDOVER

Lowe Pond

Hood Pond WSF

WILLOWDALE STATE FOREST

1b

ANDOVER

95

Boston Brook

BOXFORD SF

1x

Ipswich River

TOPSFIELD

PALMER SP

HPSF

1x

HAROLD PARKER SF

HAMILTON

TEWKSBURY

Field Pond

MIDDLETON

Putnamville Res.

Miles River

1bh

Martins Pond

Swan Pond

Middleton Pond

WENHAM

Wenham Lake

93

NORTH READING

1c

BILLERICA

WILMINGTON

1c

Peabody

1b

DANVERS

BEVERLY

LYNNFIELD

READING

PEABODY

BURLINGTON

WOBURN

N

Basin Boundary

LEGEND

LAND FEATURES

Built-up Land

Protected Land

Federal

State/Local government

Private

RIVERINE FEATURES

Dam

Hydroelectric facility

Public access

NPDES discharge sites*

CANOE RATINGS

Surface Conditions

1. Smooth
2. Mostly smooth
3. Mixed smooth and rapid

4. Mostly rapid
x. not recommended
h. Passable only in high water

Aesthetics

a. Very attractive
b. Pleasant
c. Fair

*National Pollution Discharge Elimination System Permit Sites

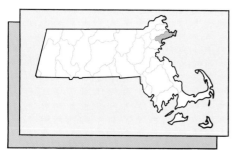

River Basin:
North Coastal

Total Drainage Area: 245 sq. mi.
Drainage Area in MA: 245 sq. mi.
River Lengths in MA:
 Essex River: 3.1 mi.
 Danvers River: 1.6 mi.
 Saugus River: 13.0 mi.
 Pines River: 3.0 mi.
 Annisquam River: 4.0 mi.
Acres of Ponds, Lakes, Reservoirs: 2,428
Features: most distinctive rocky coast in the state, Halibut Point State Park, Lynn Woods, Saugus Iron Works National Park

Rare Species:

Plants: sweetbay magnolia ●, knotted pearlwork, sea lyme-grass ●, small whorled pogonia #
Animals: least tern, common tern, spotted turtle, Mystic Valley amphipod

● Endangered in Massachusetts
Federally Endangered

North Coastal Basin

In the North Shore area, the southernmost reaches of granite from the White Mountain range can be detected, particularly right at the edge of the sea. Some of the most distinctive rocky coast in Massachusetts is found here. The rivers in this area are generally small, tidal and have historically been heavily exploited by industry. Among the rivers of interest are the Essex, the Annisquam, the Danvers, the Saugus and the Pines. These drain into the numerous harbors and bays located in the communities along the coast.

The first industries in the area were fishing related. During the 1700's, the southern half of the basin became intensely industrialized—tanneries and other factories dumped raw wastes into the rivers. The Saugus Iron Works, which is now a national park site, was one of the many factories responsible for the pollution of rivers in the colonial era. Shellfishing was prohibited as early as 1925 and has only been partially restored in recent years. Strides are being made, but considerable pollution remains an issue in this basin.

There are some significant features of this basin worth noting. The Saugus Marsh is a large (though much abused) saltwater marsh with great potential value for both marine fisheries and wildlife. Since the halting of a major highway project that was to pass through the marsh in the early 1970's, there has been growing interest in long-term protection of the remaining marsh. There are additional valuable salt marsh areas along this coastline which could be saved with the effort of concerned citizens. Although much of the southern portion of this basin is heavily developed, leaving little natural vegetation, there are still a number of rare species which survive primarily in the marshes and along the seashore.

North Coastal estuary

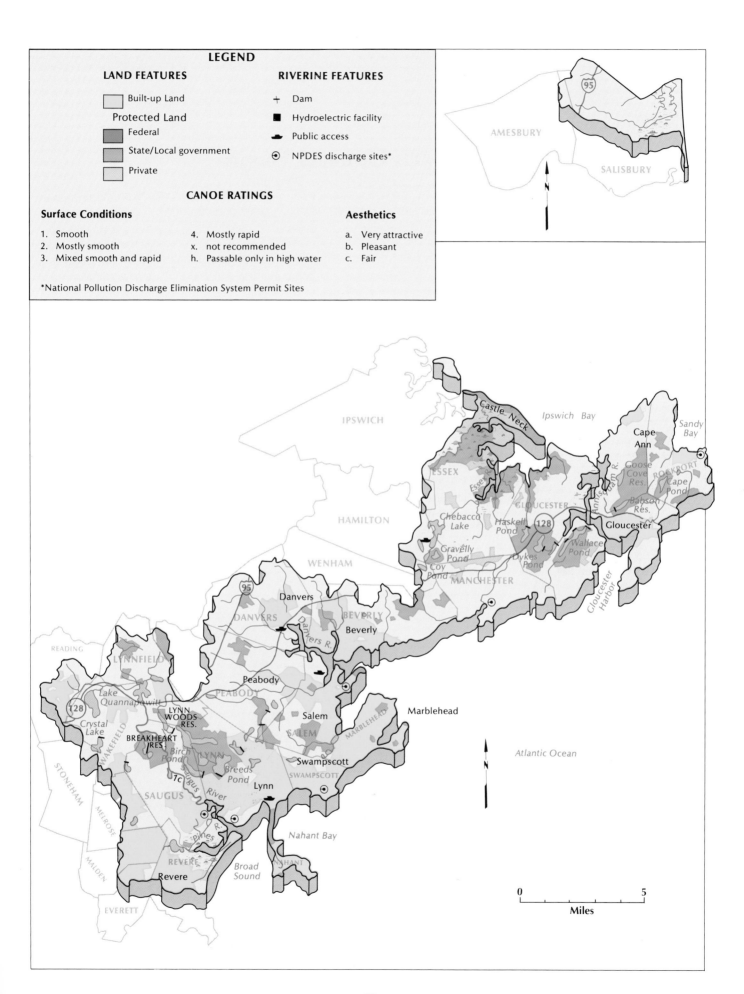

LEGEND

LAND FEATURES

Built-up Land

Protected Land

Federal

State/Local government

Private

RIVERINE FEATURES

+ Dam

■ Hydroelectric facility

Public access

⊙ NPDES discharge sites*

CANOE RATINGS

Surface Conditions

1. Smooth
2. Mostly smooth
3. Mixed smooth and rapid
4. Mostly rapid
x. not recommended
h. Passable only in high water

Aesthetics

a. Very attractive
b. Pleasant
c. Fair

*National Pollution Discharge Elimination System Permit Sites

AMESBURY

SALISBURY

IPSWICH

HAMILTON

WENHAM

Castle Neck

Ipswich Bay

Sandy Bay

Cape Ann

ESSEX

GLOUCESTER

ROCKPORT

Goose Cove Res

Cape Pond

Babson Res.

Gloucester

Chebacco Lake

Haskell Pond

Wallace Pond

Gravelly Pond

Dykes Pond

Coy Pond

MANCHESTER

Gloucester Harbor

Danvers

DANVERS

BEVERLY

Beverly

Danvers R.

READING

LYNNFIELD

Lake Quannapowitt

PEABODY

Peabody

Salem

Marblehead

Crystal Lake

LYNN WOODS RES.

SALEM

MARBLEHEAD

WAKEFIELD

BREAKHEART RES.

Birch Pond

LYNN

Breeds Pond

SWAMPSCOTT

Swampscott

STONEHAM

7c

Saugus River

Lynn

Atlantic Ocean

MELROSE

SAUGUS

Nahant Bay

MALDEN

REVERE

NAHANT

Broad Sound

Revere

EVERETT

0   5
Miles

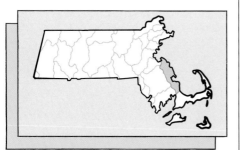

River Basin: South Coastal

Total Drainage Area: 127 sq. mi.
Drainage Area in MA: 127 sq. mi.
River Lengths in MA:
  North River: 12.0 mi.
  South River: 11.8 mi.
  Jones River: 7.4 mi.
Major Tributaries: Indian Head River, Drinkwater River
Acres of Ponds, Lakes, Reservoirs: 5,336
Features: Cape Cod Canal, Standish Monument Reservation, Plymouth Rock, cranberry bogs

Rare Species:

Plants: pale green orchis, estuary beggar's-tick ●, lesser snakeroot ●
Animals: least bittern, northern copperhead ●, banded bog skimmer dragonfly ●

● Endangered in Massachusetts

South Coastal Basin

The North River, the South River and the smaller Jones River drain into portions of the South Shore below the Boston metropolitan area. Along the coast, the area is characterized by picturesque dunes and coastal beaches. The soil is very well drained except in pockets of wet lowlands. The North and South rivers have created tidal marshes with beautiful estuaries and shining inlets. Some globally rare bird species (such as the redknot) rest and feed in the area on their annual migratory flights; others nest there. The upper North River (the freshwater portions are also called the Indian Head and Drinkwater) was once the site of bustling shipbuilding businesses. While generally a slow-moving river, it has some lively, quick-flowing sections which provide excellent canoeing. The tidal portion of the river is particularly beautiful, running through extensive marshes all the way to Massachusetts Bay.

The upper river attracts anglers and nature watchers. The landscape includes: cattails, cord grass, wild rice, cardinal flowers and wild iris. Mink, muskrat, ducks, geese and songbirds also flourish here.

The Jones River is a slower, quieter river with a distinct estuarine character in its lower reaches. Although this whole south coastal area is quite densely populated and the forest has been cut over repeatedly, its variety of open spaces still support some impressive populations of plant, invertebrate and vertebrate life. Forty-four rare species reside in the basin and state efforts to improve anadromous fisheries by repairing fish ladders are underway. However, this entire basin is facing increasing pressures from growth in year-round and summer developments which bring with them a greater need for drinking water supplies and the expanding threat posed by inadequate septic systems. At present, the Jones suffers dramatically as water from its source is diverted for water supply purposes.

The North River

Fish ladder at Curtis Pond

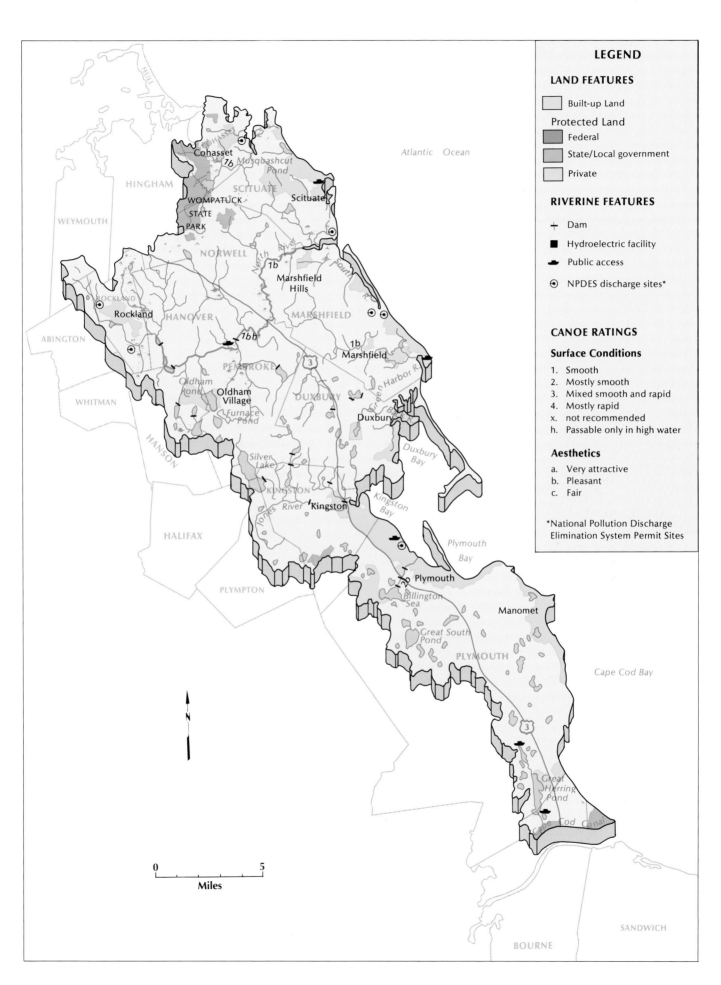

LEGEND

LAND FEATURES

Built-up Land

Protected Land

Federal

State/Local government

Private

RIVERINE FEATURES

+ Dam

■ Hydroelectric facility

Public access

⊙ NPDES discharge sites*

CANOE RATINGS

Surface Conditions

1. Smooth
2. Mostly smooth
3. Mixed smooth and rapid
4. Mostly rapid
x. not recommended
h. Passable only in high water

Aesthetics

a. Very attractive
b. Pleasant
c. Fair

*National Pollution Discharge
Elimination System Permit Sites

Atlantic Ocean

HINGHAM

WEYMOUTH

Cohasset

COHASSET

7b

Musquashcut Pond

SCITUATE

Scituate

WOMPATUCK STATE PARK

North River

NORWELL

1b

Marshfield Hills

ROCKLAND

Rockland

HANOVER

MARSHFIELD

South River

ABINGTON

1bh

PEMBROKE

3

1b

Marshfield

Green Harbor R.

WHITMAN

Oldham Pond

Oldham Village

DUXBURY

HANSON

Furnace Pond

Duxbury

Duxbury Bay

Silver Lake

KINGSTON

Jones River

Kingston

Kingston Bay

HALIFAX

Plymouth Bay

PLYMPTON

Plymouth

Billington Sea

Manomet

Great South Pond

PLYMOUTH

Cape Cod Bay

N

Great Herring Pond

3

Cape Cod Canal

SANDWICH

BOURNE

0   5

Miles

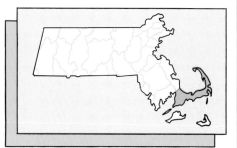

River Basin:
Cape Cod

Total Drainage Area: 422 sq. mi.
Drainage Area in MA: 422 sq. mi.
River Length in MA:
  Herring River: 6.3 mi.
Acres of Ponds, Lakes, Reservoirs:
  10,880
Features: Monomoy Island National Wildlife Refuge, Cape Cod National Seashore, Nickerson State Park, Woods Hole, Barnstable Harbor salt marshes

Rare Species:

Plants: terete arrowhead, New England boneset ●, bushy rockrose, sandplain gerardia #, heartleaf twayblade ●, salt reed-grass
Animals: piping plover +, roseate tern #, lateral bluet damselfly

● Endangered in Massachusetts
Federally Endangered
+ Federally Threatened

Cape Cod Basin

Cape Cod's 300 miles of shoreline support a tremendous variety of uses. Vacation and recreational facilities, commercial fishing, shellfishing, residential developments and wildlife habitat all make demands on the limited resources of the land. As a result, the Cape's coastal waters and rivers are showing signs of stress due to intensive use and increasing development.

Harwich's Herring River, only six miles long, is the longest river on the Cape. The small rivers in the area include the Mashpee, the Quashnet, the Pamet, the Coonamessett, the Bass, the Bumps, the Back, the Pocasett, the Red and the Swan Pond rivers. Surface runoff and inadequate septic systems account for much of the water quality problems in these small streams.

Despite stresses and disappearing habitat, many rare species are clustered on the Cape, especially in the coastal plains ponds, sandplain grasslands and heathlands. The soils on the northern (bay) side support moister conditions than the sandier soils which dominate the south coast. Some taller forests can be found in these moister sites, including areas of American holly and flowering dogwood.

Numerous fishing opportunities can be found in the area's many ponds, quite a few of which are stocked with trout. The Quashnet River is a fine example of local efforts to restore a trout steam nearly lost to changes caused by clearing, mills, cranberry bogs and other development. Local fishing enthusiasts have contributed more than 10,000 hours to cleaning the stream, improving the bottom and banks, even transplanting insects from neighboring streams to provide food for trout that now spawn in the stream once again. The eventual goal is to reintroduce the native sea run brook trout which have not been able to live in the stream for over 150 years.

Trout Unlimited and local citizens successfully lobbied the legislature for $11,000,000 to protect the Quashnet River corridor in 1987.

Trout Unlimited volunteers

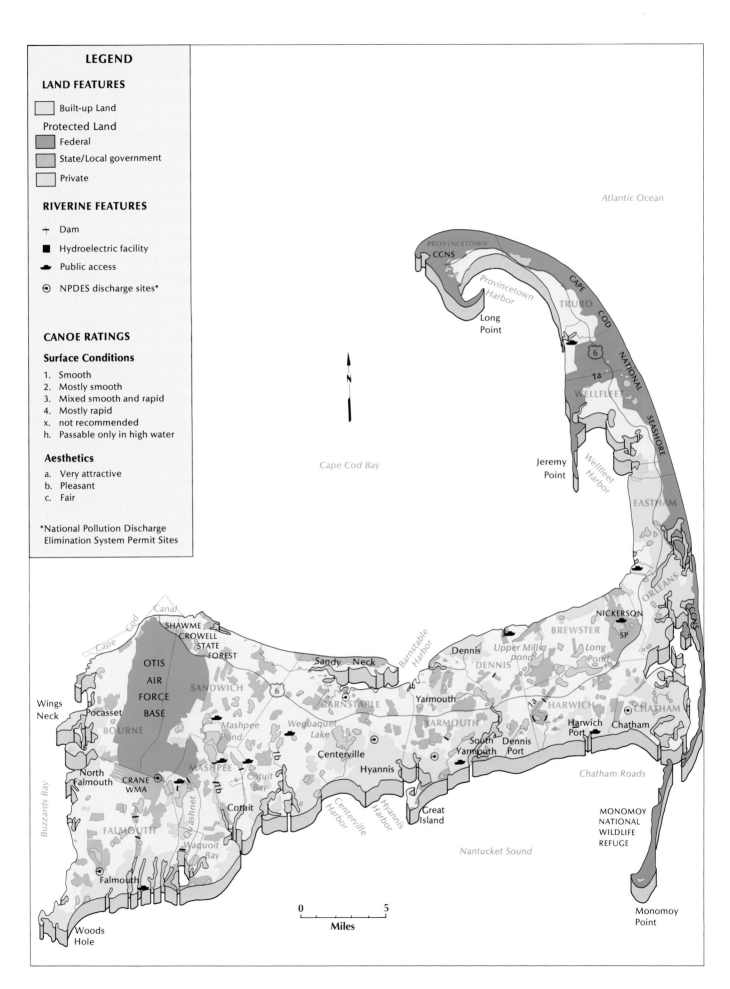

LEGEND

LAND FEATURES

Built-up Land

Protected Land

Federal

State/Local government

Private

RIVERINE FEATURES

Dam

Hydroelectric facility

Public access

NPDES discharge sites*

CANOE RATINGS

Surface Conditions

1. Smooth
2. Mostly smooth
3. Mixed smooth and rapid
4. Mostly rapid
x. not recommended
h. Passable only in high water

Aesthetics

a. Very attractive
b. Pleasant
c. Fair

*National Pollution Discharge
Elimination System Permit Sites

Atlantic Ocean

PROVINCETOWN
CCNS

Provincetown
Harbor

Long
Point

CAPE COD

TRURO

Cape Cod Bay

NATIONAL

Jeremy
Point

Wellfleet
Harbor

WELLFLEET

SEASHORE

EASTHAM

ORLEANS

CCNS

NICKERSON
SP

BREWSTER

Canal

Cape Cod

SHAWME
CROWELL
STATE
FOREST

OTIS
AIR
FORCE
BASE

SANDWICH

Sandy Neck

Barnstable Harbor

Dennis

Upper Mill
pond

Long
Pond

DENNIS

Wings
Neck

Pocasset

BOURNE

North
Falmouth

CRANE
WMA

Mashpee
Pond

MASHPEE

Quashnet

BARNSTABLE

Weequaquet
Lake

Centerville

Cotuit
Bay

Yarmouth

YARMOUTH

South
Yarmouth

Hyannis

Dennis
Port

Harwich

HARWICH

Harwich
Port

Chatham

CHATHAM

Buzzards Bay

FALMOUTH

Cotuit

Waquoit
Bay

Centerville
Harbor

Hyannis
Harbor

Great
Island

Chatham Roads

Nantucket Sound

MONOMOY
NATIONAL
WILDLIFE
REFUGE

Falmouth

Woods
Hole

0   5

Miles

Monomoy
Point

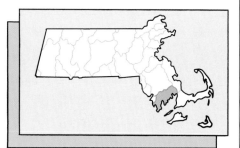

River Basin: Buzzards Bay

Total Drainage Area: 380 sq. mi.
Drainage Area in MA: 380 sq. mi.
River Lengths in MA:
  Agawam River: 6.4 mi.
  Wareham River: 2.1 mi.
  Weweantic River: 15.6 mi.
  Mattapoisett River: 9.7 mi.
  Acushnet River: 8.5 mi.
  Slocums River: 3.9 mi.
  Westport River: 3.9 mi.
Major Tributaries: East Branch
Westport, West Branch
Westport
Acres of Ponds, Lakes, Reservoirs:
6,356
Hydropower Facilities:
1; 300 kw
Features: Cape Cod Canal, Myles
Standish State Forest, Free-
town State Forest, Horseneck
Beach State Park

Rare Species:

Plants: New England boneset ●,
sandplain gerardia #, heartleaf
twayblade ●, salt reed-grass
Animals: piping plover +, roseate
tern #

●　Endangered in Massachusetts
#　Federally Endangered
+　Federally Threatened

Buzzards Bay Basin

This basin is formed by seven coastal rivers which discharge into Buzzards Bay. A number of small streams also drain into portions of the basin. The serrated coastline forms countless harbors and coves; all are popular for recreation and used for commercial fisheries.

This basin has very low elevations (average 100 feet above sea level), with sandy soils that make the uplands susceptible to droughts. Salt ponds are located along the south coast of Falmouth. Kettle hole ponds reach into the aquifer; thus, their water levels fluctuate with changes in groundwater levels. This creates special conditions needed by many rare plants and animals.

The climate is more continental than might be expected from the seaside location; in some portions frosts have been recorded every month of the year. The soil has such a low water holding capacity that rain immediately percolates through and is not available for plant growth or the decomposition of plant materials. As a result, species have adapted to low nutrient, naturally acidic and drought conditions.

There are a large variety of plant and animal species, notably the Plymouth red-bellied turtle and several species of rare moths which thrive in this region's pine barrens. The area is prone to periodic burning and many species have become adapted to fire. Good quality barrier beaches provide habitat for piping plover. There are some outstanding freshwater and tidal marshes, particularly along the Westport and Agawam rivers.

The estuarine communities along the coastal plain are now being recognized as critical to marine fisheries. Unfortunately, years of abuse and pollution, beginning in Colonial days, have left their mark and have closed thousands of acres to shellfishing. While much of the contamination appears to be limited to New Bedford Harbor, extensive studies are underway to check the extent of the problem and to begin the long process of restoring health to the fragile coastal ecosystem.

Roseate terns

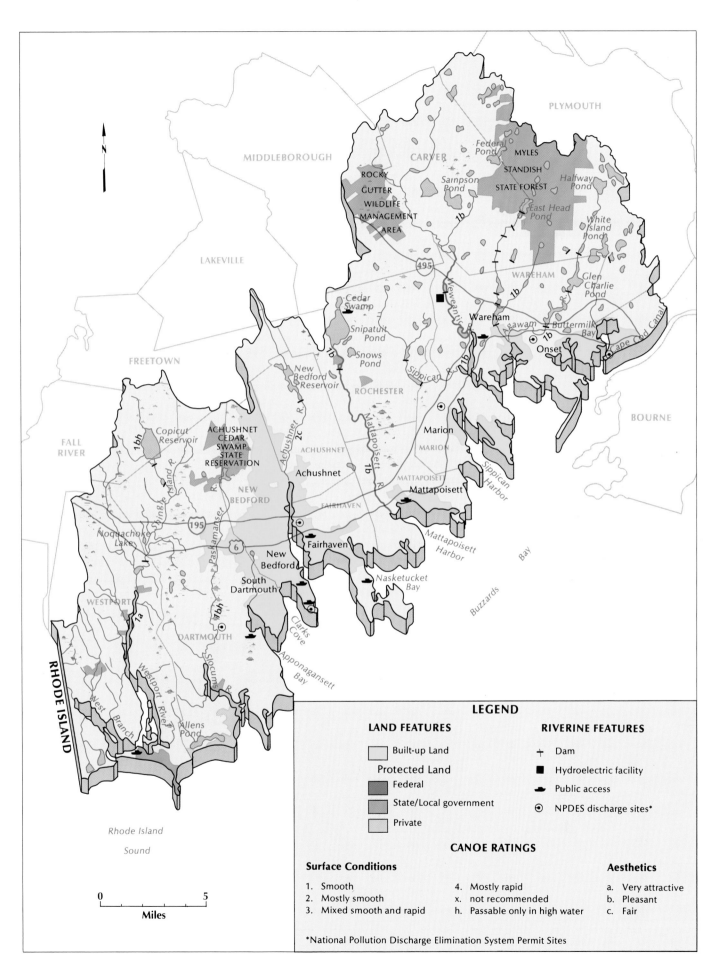

LEGEND

LAND FEATURES

Built-up Land

Protected Land

Federal

State/Local government

Private

RIVERINE FEATURES

✝ Dam

■ Hydroelectric facility

⬋ Public access

⊙ NPDES discharge sites*

CANOE RATINGS

Surface Conditions

1. Smooth
2. Mostly smooth
3. Mixed smooth and rapid

4. Mostly rapid
x. not recommended
h. Passable only in high water

Aesthetics

a. Very attractive
b. Pleasant
c. Fair

*National Pollution Discharge Elimination System Permit Sites

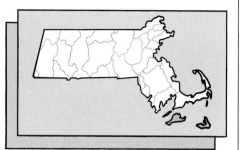

River Basin:
The Islands

Total Drainage Area: 157 sq. mi.
Drainage Area in MA:
 Elizabeth Islands: 8,300 acres
 Martha's Vineyard: 105.9 sq. mi.
 Nantucket Island: 49.5 sq. mi.
Acres of Ponds, Lakes, Reservoirs:
 7,455
Features: coastal plain ponds

Rare Species:

Plants: terete arrowhead, New
 England boneset ●, bushy rockrose, sandplain gerardia #, heartleaf twayblade ●, salt reed-
 grass
Animals: piping plover +, roseate
 tern #, lateral bluet damselfly

● Endangered in Massachusetts
\# Federally Endangered
+ Federally Threatened

The Islands—Nantucket, Martha's Vineyard & Elizabeth Islands

Located off the southern coast of Cape Cod, the Islands are part of the Atlantic Coastal Plain. The largest island off the coast of New England, Martha's Vineyard, has six towns, a 125-mile coastline and reaches an elevation of only 130 feet at its highest point. The island's extremely varied topography includes wide barrier beaches, brackish coastal ponds, outwash plains, rolling moraines and coastal cliffs. This variety in land and water forms, coupled with productive sea waters and nearness to bird migration routes, allows Martha's Vineyard to host a wide diversity of wildlife. In addition, the soils of Martha's Vineyard support post oak and tupelo trees which are not commonly found in other areas of Massachusetts.

In 1975, the entire island of Nantucket was included in the National Historical Register because of its unique architecture and its historical value. Nantucket Island has 94 miles of coastline, a maximum elevation of about 100 feet and supports the tupelo tree in its lowlands. Nantucket is also completely free of industrial wastewater discharges.

One family owns and manages all but two of the fifteen islands that make up the Elizabeth Islands chain. Cuttyhunk and Penikese islands are the exceptions. Most of the islands are grassy with areas of low woods or shrub growth, and many southern tupelos grow in the lowlands.

Each of these islands faces water supply problems, especially during tourist season. With no large rivers, the only source of freshwater supplies are ponds, and the only source of drinking water is the groundwater. However, life on the islands is dominated more by ocean waters than freshwater. All of the islands have been included under the Commonwealth's Ocean Sanctuaries Statutes which prohibit dumping, new discharges of wastes and the removal of sand or gravel.

Piping plover

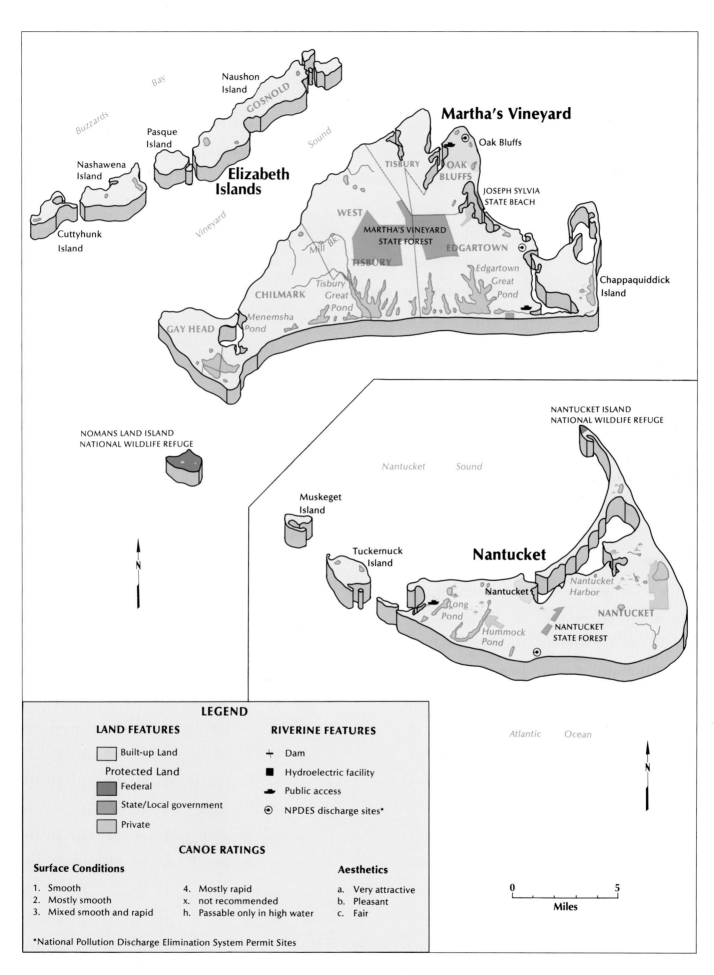

Martha's Vineyard

Buzzards Bay

Naushon Island

GOSNOLD

Pasque Island

Nashawena Island

Elizabeth Islands

Cuttyhunk Island

Vineyard Sound

TISBURY

OAK BLUFFS

Oak Bluffs

JOSEPH SYLVIA STATE BEACH

WEST TISBURY

MARTHA'S VINEYARD STATE FOREST

EDGARTOWN

Mill Bk.

CHILMARK

Tisbury Great Pond

Edgartown Great Pond

Chappaquiddick Island

GAY HEAD

Menemsha Pond

NOMANS LAND ISLAND NATIONAL WILDLIFE REFUGE

NANTUCKET ISLAND NATIONAL WILDLIFE REFUGE

Nantucket Sound

Muskeget Island

Tuckernuck Island

Nantucket

Nantucket Harbor

Nantucket

NANTUCKET

Long Pond

Hummock Pond

NANTUCKET STATE FOREST

N

Atlantic Ocean

N

0   5
Miles

LEGEND

LAND FEATURES

☐ Built-up Land

Protected Land

■ Federal

■ State/Local government

☐ Private

RIVERINE FEATURES

╈ Dam

■ Hydroelectric facility

⬧ Public access

⊙ NPDES discharge sites*

CANOE RATINGS

Surface Conditions

1. Smooth
2. Mostly smooth
3. Mixed smooth and rapid

4. Mostly rapid
x. not recommended
h. Passable only in high water

Aesthetics

a. Very attractive
b. Pleasant
c. Fair

*National Pollution Discharge Elimination System Permit Sites

V. AN INTERNATIONALLY RECOGNIZED SUCCESS STORY: THE NASHUA RIVER BASIN

Overview

Early native Americans inhabited the valley, fished for salmon and called the area "the Nashua" or "the meeting of the rivers." Later, European settlers delighted in the river as a "thing of beauty" and a "joy forever," according to local history. Early industry built dams and used the river to turn their waterwheels. In Fitchburg and nearby towns, mills were constructed for the processing of wood, wool and cotton. In time, riverside businesses dumped sawdust and vile wastes; households added their pollution. The Nashua was a fast-moving river and a seemingly effective sewer system.

Business boomed. During the Civil War, the river would turn indigo from the dyes used to make Union army uniforms. During the following century, expansion of towns and factories led to dumping of more waste and sewage. The color of the river changed—red, white, blue or green—depending on the dyes used by the paper mills. In the absence of dyes, it was a putrid grey, and people used to bet on what color the water would be on a given day. Heavy metals mixed with the sediments; the river was sluggish with waste. Oxygen was depleted. The Nashua became "too thick to pour, too thin to plow"—and by the early 1960's, it was practically dead. Clogged with trash, the stench was intolerable, and sewage worms were the chief form of aquatic life. Some people suggested covering the worst sections with pavement.

However, a few people in the Nashua valley had a grander vision. In the 1960's, they began a campaign against the long history of abuse. The campaign to save a river gradually grew into a basin-wide conservation effort; twenty-five years later, it was recognized by the United Nations Environment Programme as a model for environmental effectiveness.

Marion Stoddart played the key role in mapping out that grander vision for the river. Through her efforts, the Nashua River Cleanup Committee was organized. The two major objectives of the committee were to restore the Nashua as a scenic river and to protect land along the riverbanks as a "greenway" for wildlife, recreation and other purposes.

The committee pressed leaders in business and government to stop the pollution. They won mayors over to the cause,

petitioned the governor and took a U.S. senator for a canoe tour. The press often featured this dedicated group that took on a task most people had considered impossible. Eventually, the committee gained the support of the paper companies, labor unions and others who initially had opposed an environmental cleanup. These groups had mistakenly feared that it might cost jobs and cause an economic downturn for the region.

1965 - before citizen action

1987 - after citizen action

In 1969, the cleanup committee was incorporated as the non-profit Nashua River Watershed Association (NRWA). Marion Stoddart foresaw that the job required a diverse constituency which would advocate for the river's protection in the long run. She knew that the price of a quality environment was "constant vigilance." The NRWA dreamed of someday accomplishing two grand goals:

—restoring the Nashua to fishable and swimmable status; and

—preserving the wild land along its banks as a permanently protected "greenway" valued by valley residents.

Over the years, tremendous strides have been made. Five new sewage treatment plants have removed 90% of the pollutants, and the river flows nearly clean. Fish have returned in abundance and people enjoy canoeing the river's winding course. The greenway stretches to protect nearly two-thirds of the riverfront lands—almost 7,000 acres. The Nashua and two of its tributaries—the Squannacook and the Stillwater—have been designated as scenic rivers by the state.

The Nashua River corridor now attracts deer, fox, coyote, beaver, otter and other mammals that rely on the greenway corridor for daily needs such as food, water, cover and travel routes. In addition, a rich diversity of other fauna and flora inhabit the greenway corridor. This river corridor also links large open spaces (three state forests, two state reservations, a national wildlife refuge and several local conservation areas) and protects the most environmentally fragile portions of the Nashua valley. This corridor can function as a sustainable ecosystem as long as zoning and land use patterns in the region do not change substantially. River corridor protection fulfills many of the principles of landscape ecology and preserves a river basin's natural community of wildlife and flora.

However, the Nashua River restoration is not complete. There are problems with sewage overflows, heavy metals in the sediments and malfunctioning treatment plants. The greenway does not yet stretch along the whole length of the river, nor is the river swimmable. Careless development and waste disposal problems are on-going threats to the region's water quality and to the quality of life in the area, but the Nashua is no longer "too thick to pour, too thin to plow."

The river stood out as an eyesore in the 1960's. It stands out today for a very different reason; it is a shining example of what dedicated citizens, in partnership with private industry and government agencies, can accomplish when they decide to put an end to environmental abuse.

Snowy egret

Red fox

Autumn splendor

River Corridor Protection—
A Plan with Many Purposes

In the front of this book opposite the title page is a map that blueprints the quality of our environment in Massachusetts; the 28 river basins shown are the major ecosystems of the state. The basin maps (in section IV) show that the lifelines of these natural divisions are the rivers and their adjacent corridors. The map of a section of the Nashua River on the facing page shows the benefits that result when many interests with different objectives pool their efforts to conserve riparian corridors.

For example:
—Bolton Flats Wildlife Management Area - This 923 acre parcel protects four miles of riverfront. The northern part was first acquired by The Nature Conservancy in 1977 with the help of the Nashua River Watershed Association. This area and additional parcels were then purchased by the state with funds from hunting license fees. Ten years later, the southern part was transferred to the Division of Corrections.

Much of the fertile river bottom lands are leased to farmers who, as part of their lease agreement, leave a portion of their crops to feed wildlife. The Division of Fisheries and Wildlife stock pheasant in the fall for hunting enjoyment. Many animals thrive on the reserve, and the area is a favorite spot for bird watching and nature walks. A check-off list of 212 bird species sighted there may be obtained from the Division of Fisheries and Wildlife. Adding to the state lands, the Town of Lancaster has acquired an abutting 20 acres for a parking area and a canoe launch.

—North Nashua Conservation Area - Several abutting parcels acquired at different times by state and local agencies now protect 695 open space acres along 5 miles of the North Nashua River in Leominster and Lancaster. The area offers many forms of outdoor recreation and has also preserved much of the original homestead of the well-known folk hero, Johnny Appleseed. In addition, a developer is donating 27 acres of abutting land to the greenway. The gift will benefit both the river corridor ecosystem and add to the value of the new homes in the development.

—The Wachusett Reservoir is a key link in the greater Boston water supply. To provide a protective buffer, the Metropolitan District Commission has established a large conservation area around the reservoir. Both add enormously to the quality of life in nearby towns. The reservation keeps wildlife habitat and outdoor recreation close at hand, and the reservoir is a popular fishing spot that yields many trophy-class fish.

All three areas demonstrate the many benefits that protected river corridors can provide for fisheries, wildlife, agriculture, water supplies and recreation.

Protection Techniques: Two federal, five state and four town agencies in six towns own and protect portions of the Nashua greenway shown on the map. Conservation agreements granted by private owners to local conservation commissions protect other stretches of the river. In 1986, the Town of Sterling enacted a zoning setback (no-build area) along the Stillwater River. Local floodplain zoning and the state wetlands law also help to protect the Nashua River corridor.

Historic Preservation: Along with environmental values, river corridors usually have a rich history. Johnny Appleseed was born and grew up along the North Nashua. Benton MacKaye, the founder of the Appalachian Trail, lived in Shirley, wandered the river's course and wrote extensively about it. On February 13, 1675, Metacomet (King Philip), burned the bridges crossing the Nashua River and struck a deadly raid on the early settlement of Lancaster. In Harvard, the experimental commune and home of Bronson Alcott is now the site of the Fruitlands Museum. Fruitlands also contains many acres of wildlife habitat that abut the Oxbow National Wildlife Reserve. Also located near this stretch of the Nashua River greenway is the birthplace of renowned plant breeder Luther Burbank.

Frozen marshlands

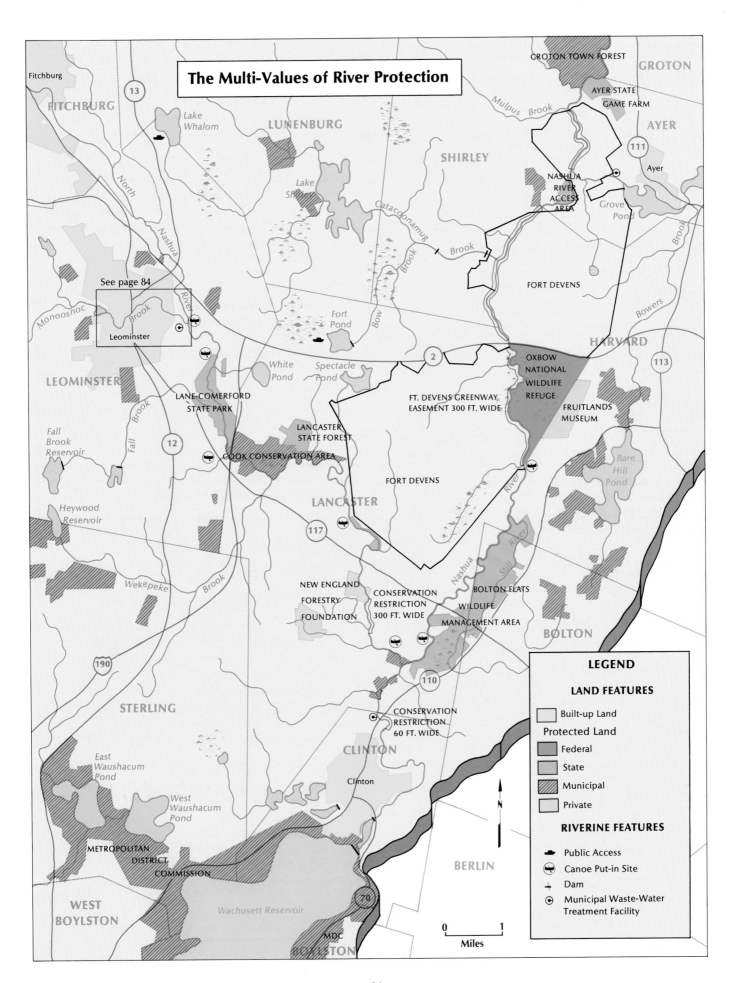

The Multi-Values of River Protection

Fitchburg

FITCHBURG

GROTON TOWN FOREST

GROTON

13

Lake Whalom

LUNENBURG

AYER STATE GAME FARM

AYER

Mulpus Brook

111

Ayer

SHIRLEY

NASHUA RIVER ACCESS AREA

Grove Pond

Lake Shirley

Cataccdonamug Brook

North Nashua River

Brook

See page 84

Leominster

Brook

Bow Brook

Fort Pond

FORT DEVENS

HARVARD

113

Monoosnoc Brook

2

OXBOW NATIONAL WILDLIFE REFUGE

FRUITLANDS MUSEUM

White Pond

Spectacle Pond

FT. DEVENS GREENWAY EASEMENT 300 FT. WIDE

Bowers Brook

LEOMINSTER

LANE-COMERFORD STATE PARK

Fall Brook

LANCASTER STATE FOREST

Fall Brook Reservoir

12

COOK CONSERVATION AREA

FORT DEVENS

Bare Hill Pond

River

Heywood Reservoir

LANCASTER

Nashua River

Still River

117

Wekepeke Brook

NEW ENGLAND FORESTRY FOUNDATION

CONSERVATION RESTRICTION 300 FT. WIDE

BOLTON FLATS WILDLIFE MANAGEMENT AREA

BOLTON

190

STERLING

110

CONSERVATION RESTRICTION 60 FT. WIDE

East Waushacum Pond

CLINTON

West Waushacum Pond

Clinton

METROPOLITAN DISTRICT COMMISSION

BERLIN

WEST BOYLSTON

70

Wachusett Reservoir

MDC BOYLSTON

LEGEND

LAND FEATURES

- Built-up Land

Protected Land

- Federal
- State
- Municipal
- Private

RIVERINE FEATURES

- Public Access
- Canoe Put-in Site
- Dam
- Municipal Waste-Water Treatment Facility

N

0   1
Miles

Adopt-A-Stream Citizen Group

The Nashua experience has demonstrated how citizens can achieve near miracles in environmental restoration. The strategy and methods used by the Nashua River Watershed Association can be successfully applied by any group trying to revitalize any river or stream.

The facing page outlines the Adopt-A-Stream (AAS) Program that was developed by the Massachusetts Department of Fisheries, Wildlife & Environmental Law Enforcement. The program, which has over 350 participants, is designed to assist people who want to improve and protect waterways in their communities.

The AAS Program is based on effective methods used by river and stream protection organizations. These organizations include the Nashua River Watershed Association, the Charles River Watershed Association, the Izaak Walton League of America Save Our Streams Program, the Pennsylvania Fish Commission's Adopt-A-Stream Program, and Trout Unlimited's Embrace-A-Stream Program.

Adopt-A-Stream shows how citizen groups can take a grand vision (such as fishable / swimmable protected river corridors) and establish long-term goals. These goals can then guide more specific objectives, as well as provide easily-understood and do-able actions. People may often be overwhelmed or discouraged by the challenge of restoring a neglected river. AAS teaches people how to start out small and build; one act kindles another. For example, a newly formed group could begin by organizing a trash removal day or a canoe tour. These tasks create awareness and attract aditional help for tackling more complex issues of river corridor protection.

Many river restoration actions require funding and the backing of local, state or federal governments. It is important to note that citizen groups usually lack legal authority, nor do they have direct access to funding for wastewater treatment or land acquisition. Instead, they have tremendous power to create public awareness and advocate for actions by the agencies that do have authority and funds. As expressed by Rita Barron of the Charles River Watershed Association, "local citizen groups have credibility with neighborhood landowners, local officials and media . . . they have the power of cooperation with minimum conflict." Even uncooperative officials and agencies will respond to an effective group which is working in a responsible manner for the public good. Advocacy is the most important function a citizen river-watch group can perform.

Citizen advocates can provide river corridor landowners with information on proper land use practices. They can also identify landowners who are willing to donate or sell river corridor lands to private environmental organizations or public agencies.

The legal authority needed to protect rivers and enforce environmental laws often rests with local government. Municipal decisions are the key to environmental protecton today. Yet, few towns fully realize or appreciate the value and responsibility of their growth management authority. In his Community Report Card for Environmental Protection '86 noted environmental attorney Gregor I. McGregor argues,

"Do not expect comprehensive federal and state legislation to bail you out of problems with threats of groundwater contamination, watershed development aggravating flood damages, dwindling open space and recreation resources, suburban sprawl, strip development, industrial pollution, or ugly buildings. Do not wait for Washington or the State House. Create environmental law on your own terms tailored to your community."

Adopt-A-Stream used McGregor's "report card" to help guide concerned citizens in evaluating the adequacy of their community's bylaws and regulations for protecting river corridors. As part of this process, AAS offers model river protection bylaws for consideration by towns.

River Corridors Need Partnerships

No single public agency has the authority to stop pollution and conserve river corridors. It takes partnerships among public agencies, non-profit organizations, business and industry to protect our rivers. Local watershed associations play a key role in building the partnerships with all these groups.

As the river is protected, a watershed association can reach out to bring about additional improvements. State fish and wildlife experts are often willing to suggest ways to improve stream habitat. Trout Unlimited, a national organization, may provide assistance and funding for trout stream improvements when asked by a watershed association.

The size and abilities of a citizen group should match the size and complexity of the problems. A small neighborhood group will be able to adopt a short segment of a brook if the only need is to clean up litter and improve fish and wildlife habitat. Restoring a major river such as the Nashua may be started by a local cleanup committee, but eventually will require an organization with non-profit status for fundraising purposes and for hiring staff with environmental expertise.

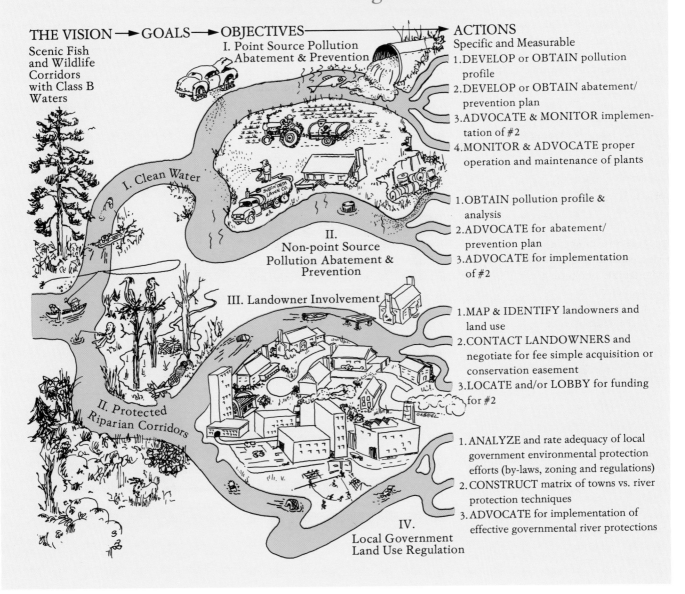

Adopt a Stream
Program

THE VISION → GOALS → OBJECTIVES ─────── ACTIONS

THE VISION
Scenic Fish and Wildlife Corridors with Class B Waters

GOALS
I. Clean Water
II. Protected Riparian Corridors

OBJECTIVES

I. Point Source Pollution Abatement & Prevention

II. Non-point Source Pollution Abatement & Prevention

III. Landowner Involvement

IV. Local Government Land Use Regulation

ACTIONS
Specific and Measurable

1. DEVELOP or OBTAIN pollution profile
2. DEVELOP or OBTAIN abatement/prevention plan
3. ADVOCATE & MONITOR implementation of #2
4. MONITOR & ADVOCATE proper operation and maintenance of plants

1. OBTAIN pollution profile & analysis
2. ADVOCATE for abatement/prevention plan
3. ADVOCATE for implementation of #2

1. MAP & IDENTIFY landowners and land use
2. CONTACT LANDOWNERS and negotiate for fee simple acquisition or conservation easement
3. LOCATE and/or LOBBY for funding for #2

1. ANALYZE and rate adequacy of local government environmental protection efforts (by-laws, zoning and regulations)
2. CONSTRUCT matrix of towns vs. river protection techniques
3. ADVOCATE for implementation of effective governmental river protections

The Value of Greenways in an Urban Setting—Monoosnoc Brook

Leominster literally grew up along Monoosnoc Brook, a tributary of the Nashua River. Industry drew waterpower, and the city became a major plastics manufacturing center. However, the life pumped into the industrial sector took its toll on the vitality of the brook which suffered from neglect and pollution.

The Leominster business community, city officials and the watershed association are the driving forces behind a team effort to reclaim a neglected brook and revitalize the downtown area of this old industrial city.

In 1987, a public-private coalition formed to change the situation. The Monoosnoc Brook Greenway Project is a partnership between business and industry, local government, citizens and the Mayor's coalition for the Monoosnoc Brook. The Nashua River Watershed Association gives guidance and technical assistance when needed. Progress is being made in cleaning up the brook, and in designing an urban greenway along the section of the brook which flows through the downtown area. The 1988 cleanup yielded over eight truckloads of debris from the brook. Fortunately, no major sources of industrial waste enter the brook.

The landscape design includes a walking path behind Searstown Mall, tree plantings, benches and mini-parks. The city is proud of restoring the brook and the restoration has instilled a new sense of pride in the community.

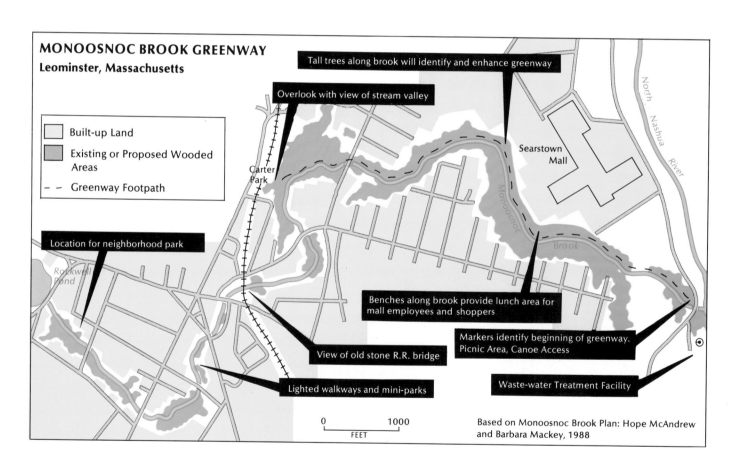

MONOOSNOC BROOK GREENWAY
Leominster, Massachusetts

Built-up Land

Existing or Proposed Wooded Areas

– – Greenway Footpath

Tall trees along brook will identify and enhance greenway

Overlook with view of stream valley

Searstown Mall

Carter Park

Location for neighborhood park

Rockwell Pond

Benches along brook provide lunch area for mall employees and shoppers

View of old stone R.R. bridge

Markers identify beginning of greenway. Picnic Area, Canoe Access

Lighted walkways and mini-parks

Waste-water Treatment Facility

North Nashua River

Monoosnoc Brook

0   1000
FEET

Based on Monoosnoc Brook Plan: Hope McAndrew and Barbara Mackey, 1988

VI. CONCLUSION

Regenerated forests, open meadows, marshes, cleaner rivers and an exceptional diversity of fish, wildlife, plants, and natural communities today provide Massachusetts' citizens with a greater natural heritage than at any time in the past two centuries.

But this heritage now faces a much greater threat than that posed by any of the agricultural and industrial development which has taken place in Massachusetts since the Pilgrims landed. Today, the short-sighted, speculative development trend of the 1980's (see graph and narrative on page 19) poses an irreversible threat to the character of the land and to wildlife. Unfortunately, government alone cannot prevent the inevitable environmental and socioeconomic costs of ongoing, uncoordinated development patterns.

If environmental problems are to be remedied and prevented, a broad constituency of concerned and informed citizens is essential. Private, non-profit watershed associations have discovered that teaching the concepts of river basins as the ecological units of the state and riparian corridors as the lifelines of those units is the most effective means of informing citizens about ecological principles and problems. While people today feel overwhelmed by global environmental problems, river corridor restoration and protection provides them with an ideal opportunity to solve environmental problems at the local level.

River and stream corridor restoration and protection is not a panacea for environmental salvation. It is, however, an endeavor in which virtually every interest group—from bird watchers to developers—can work together to protect the most vital ecological areas in the state.

Through environmental education and awareness about river corridor protection, citizens learn that careful development is needed throughout each river basin in order to protect our great natural heritage. By working in partnership with non-profits and other area residents, private landowners, developers, businesses and local governments can achieve their economic goals while preserving the integrity of the land and the state's ecological infrastructure.

A corporate canoe trip on the Assabet River.

VII. LIST OF WATERSHED ASSOCIATIONS AND REFERENCES

Organization for the ASSABET RIVER
Damonmill Square
Concord, MA 01742

BLACKSTONE RIVER Watershed Association
P.O. Box 96
Whitinsville, MA 01588

CANOE RIVER Aquifer Committee
25 Eastman Avenue
Foxboro, MA 02035

CHARLES RIVER Watershed Association
2391 Commonwealth Avenue
Auburndale, MA 02166

CHICOPEE RIVER Watershed Council
P.O. Box 148
Chicopee, MA 01014

CONNECTICUT RIVER Watershed Council
125 Combs Road
Easthampton, MA 01027

DEERFIELD RIVER Watershed Association
P.O. Box 13
Shelburne Falls, MA 01370

DESTRUCTION BROOK
Friends of Russells Mills
P.O. Box 13
Dartmouth, MA 02714

FARMINGTON RIVER Watershed Association
749 Hop Meadow Street
Simsbury, CT 06070

Friends of FISH BROOK
20 Cross Street
Boxford, MA 01921

GREEN RIVER Watershed Preservation Alliance
P.O. Box 398
Leyden, MA 01337

HOOSIC RIVER Watershed Association
P.O. Box 268
North Adams, MA 01247

HOUSATONIC RIVER Watershed Association
Planning Dept. - City Hall
70 Allen Street
Pittsfield, MA 01202

IPSWICH RIVER Watershed Association
87 Perkins Row
Topsfield, MA 01937

JONES RIVER Watershed Association
42 Landing Road
Kingston, MA 02364

LAMPSON BROOK Watershed Association
N.E. Small Farm Institute
P.O. Box 937
Belchertown, MA 01007

MERRIMACK RIVER Watershed Council
Civil Defense Building
694 Main Street
West Newbury, MA 01985

MILLERS RIVER Watershed Council
P.O. Box 23
Athol, MA 01331

MYSTIC RIVER Watershed Association
276 Massachusetts Ave. #510
Arlington, MA 02174

NASHUA RIVER Watershed Association
P.O. Box 7613
Fitchburg, MA 01420

NEPONSET RIVER Watershed Association
293 Moosehill Street
Sharon, MA 02067

NORTH & SOUTH RIVERS Watershed Association
P.O. Box 43
Norwell, MA 02061

OLD SWAMP RIVER
South Weymouth Neighborhood Association
P.O. Box 478
South Weymouth, MA 02190